Dear Reader:

The book you are about to read is the latest bestseller from the St. Martin's True Crime Library, the imprint *The New York Times* calls "the leader in true crime!" Each month, we offer you a fascinating account of the latest, most sensational crime that has captured the national attention. St. Martin's is the publisher of Tina Dirmann's VANISHED AT SEA, the story of a former child actor who posed as a yacht buyer in order to lure an older couple out to sea, then robbed them and threw them overboard to their deaths. John Glatt's riveting and horrifying SECRETS IN THE CELLAR shines a light on the man who shocked the world when it was revealed that he had kept his daughter locked in his hidden basement for 24 years. In the Edgar-nominated WRITTEN IN BLOOD, Diane Fanning looks at Michael Petersen, a Marine-turned-novelist found guilty of beating his wife to death and pushing her down the stairs of their home—only to reveal another similar death from his past. In the book you now hold, MURDER AT YALE, Stella Sands examines a recent case of murder that has attracted national headlines.

St. Martin's True Crime Library gives you the stories behind the headlines. Our authors take you right to the scene of the crime and into the minds of the most notorious murderers to show you what really makes them tick. St. Martin's True Crime Library paperbacks are better than the most terrifying thriller, because it's all true! The next time you want a crackling good read, make sure it's got the St. Martin's True Crime Library logo on the spine—you'll be up all night!

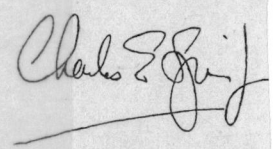

Charles E. Spicer, Jr.
Executive Editor, St. Martin's True Crime Library

TITLES BY STELLA SANDS

Behind the Mask

Murder at Yale

from the True Crime Library of St. Martin's Paperbacks

MURDER AT YALE

STELLA SANDS

St. Martin's Paperbacks

MURDER AT YALE

Copyright © 2010 by Stella Sands.

Cover photo of Raymond Clark by Douglas Healey–Pool/Getty Images. Photo of Yale University building courtesy of visitNewHaven.com. Photo of gates by Richard Nowitz/Getty Images.

For information address St. Martin's Press, 175 Fifth Avenue, New York, NY 10010.

EAN: 978-0-312-53164-5

Printed in the United States of America

St. Martin's Paperbacks edition / July 2010

St. Martin's Paperbacks are published by St. Martin's Press, 175 Fifth Avenue, New York, NY 10010.

10 9 8 7 6 5 4 3 2 1

NOV 07 2011

For Sass, somewhere over the rainbow

ACKNOWLEDGMENTS

At the time of the writing of this book, a trial date had not yet been set for Raymond Clark. As a result, many of those most closely involved with the case—the police, lawyers, family, and friends—could not speak to me. However, I did have fruitful and eye-opening discussions with attorney Glenn Conway, to whom I owe a huge debt of gratitude. I would like to thank Michael Welner, MD, for generously taking the time to analyze the case and offering his penetrating insights.

Thank yous also to Margaret Mittelbach for her perceptive comments on the manuscript; to Jennifer Dixon for her discerning eye and constant support; and to Marjorie Frank and Pablo Serrano for their hugs and encouragement.

To my agent Giles Anderson, to Executive Editor Charlie Spicer, to Editor Allison Caplin, and to copy editor Katherine Pradt, an enormous and heartfelt thank you.

And to Jess and AF, for being who they are, always.

It was violent. It was bloody. And it was deadly.

At prestigious Yale University.
In a soundproof basement lab of a medical school building.
Annie Marie Le, a twenty-four-year-old graduate student.
Murdered on September 8, 2009.

No doubt, there were words. Then uncontrollable rage.

Blood in basement lab rooms told the story—but for days, Annie Le's fate remained a mystery . . . .

PART
I

ONE

The story of Annie Marie Le's disappearance grabbed the nation by the gut—and from the very beginning, it was a mystery that boded ill.

It began quietly enough. When Le didn't come home on the night of Tuesday, September 8, 2009, her roommate called the Yale Police Department to report that Le, a grad student at the university, had seemingly disappeared.

By Wednesday, word swirled around campus. *Where could Annie Le have gone? Was she out partying somewhere? Wait . . . wasn't she engaged? Do you think someone did something to her?*

On Thursday, September 10, the *Yale Daily News* published an article: "Graduate Student Goes Missing." That same day, NYDailyNews.com reported: "Yale grad student Annie Le disappears 5 days before New York wedding."

On Friday, September 11, the search for Le began heating up in earnest, along with a tumult of media. The *New Haven Independent* (an online local news site) reported a "$10,000 Reward Posted in Annie Le Case."

By then, the police had officially labeled Annie Le a "missing person."

Across the country that morning, the TV screamed the news. In the critical first half hour of their morning broadcasts, CBS, NBC, and ABC focused their reporting on the circumstances surrounding Le's disappearance. The major networks not only reported from their studios in New York, but they also sent camera crews and reporters to the Yale campus to interview students and faculty.

At 7:01 a.m., on NBC's *Today* show, Matt Lauer discussed Le's disappearance as the second leading story of the day. Then, after moving on to the health care debate taking place in Washington, *Today* returned to the Yale campus at 7:08 a.m. with more on the missing student. No one who knew Le could offer a single clue as to where she might be. NBC reporter Jeff Rossen went so far as to utter the unthinkable: "Annie Le may be the victim of a violent crime."

At 7:18 a.m., *Good Morning America* broadcast live from Yale, and in a segment on the case, told about the deep love and friendship that existed between Le and her fiancé, Jon Widawsky of Long Island, New York. The program put on view stunningly happy photos of the two from Facebook.

At 7:21 a.m., CBS reporters told about the disappearance of the grad student, but saved a fuller segment for the *Early Show*. The cameras scanned the Yale campus, honing in on 10 Amistad Street, where Le was last seen. Back in the studio, a reporter interviewed Pat Brown, a criminal profiler, who opined that it was "interesting" that the authorities were stating that they did not suspect foul play. As to rumors that Le could be a runaway bride, Brown said that brides-to-be who run off typically have an attention-getting personality, and if Le "doesn't have that kind of personality, then we'd have to suspect foul play because *what else could it be?*"

As the day and news reports wore on, so did the mystery. No one knew where Annie Le was—and no one knew what had happened to her.

On Saturday, there was a possible break in the case. The *Hartford Courant* reported, "Bloody Clothes Found in Yale Building During Search for Missing Student." The *New York Times* weighed in with this headline: "Items Seized in Search for Yale Student Who Disappeared Days before Wedding." Other news media picked up the story, and the frenzy of hearsay and speculation grew only louder as the mystery congealed.

Late in the afternoon on Sunday, September 13, the police and news media dropped a bombshell. Annie Le had been located. There wasn't going to be any wedding. No rings or vows would be exchanged. Her friends would never catch her bouquet as she excitedly tossed it over her shoulder.

The body of Annie Le was found stuffed into a wall in the basement lab where she worked, at 10 Amistad Street.

She was a homicide victim.

During the week of September 14, 2009, a virtual tsunami of media coverage engulfed the public. Only Barack Obama was featured in more news stories in the United States than Annie Le. In death, Le became a media obsession. In life, she had been a classic American success story and inspiration—the daughter of hardworking immigrants, Le had studied fiercely, followed her dreams, and planned to devote her career to helping others. How could something so terrible have happened to her? And how could such a callous and apparently brutal murder have taken place in the hushed and hallowed halls of Yale University? The walls of this fortress of scholarship and polite discourse had been breached by some unnamed evil. And if evil could worm its way into the cocoon of a place like Yale, was there anywhere it couldn't reach? All across America, people who followed the news of Le's disappearance and death were searching for answers.

TWO

Annie Le (pronounced LAY) was both brilliant and beautiful—enrolled in the highly selective pharmacology program at Yale's Medical School. She had worked like the dickens to get to the Ivy League. And her success there, as a woman, as a minority (her heritage was Vietnamese) was one of countless emblems of how Yale had progressed from its early beginnings.

Yale University stretches across hundreds of acres like a royal forest and back in time with a distinctive lineage. Although not reserved for a monarch or the aristocracy, the university is nevertheless a haven for the privileged.

Founded in 1701 in the British colony of Connecticut, Yale was originally named the Collegiate School "wherein Youth may be instructed in the Arts and Sciences [and] through the blessing of Almighty God may be fitted for Publick employment both in Church and Civil State."

The Collegiate School became Yale College in 1718, after it received a donation from Elihu Yale, a Welsh merchant and governor of the British East India Company. His gift included the proceeds of nine bales of goods, 417 books, and a portrait of King George.

Today, Yale is considered one of the foremost universities in the country, always ranked among the top five, if not the top two or number one. While its student body was originally restricted to a handful of white men, it now boasts more than 11,000 students, approximately half of which are women and 30 percent are people of color.

Made up of 260 historic buildings in styles ranging from Georgian to Neo-Gothic to contemporary, with many of the newer buildings designed by distinguished architects from all over the world—Eero Saarinen's Ingalls Rink, Louis Kahn's Yale Art Gallery and Center for British Art, and Paul Rudolph's Art & Architecture Building, to name a few—each a stunning standout in the canons of architectural achievements. Yale is also among the most beautiful urban campuses in America. Noteworthy buildings with stone sculptures in their walls, decorative friezes, towering gates, majestic arches, tree-lined walkways, and expansive courtyards and lawns make Yale a campus to behold.

Located in New Haven, which current Yale president Richard C. Levin noted was "large enough to be interesting, yet small enough to be friendly," the university boasts many distinguished alumni, including five U.S. presidents (William Howard Taft, Gerald Ford, George H. W. Bush, Bill Clinton, and George W. Bush); other politicos who made serious bids for the presidency, including Hillary Rodham Clinton, Howard Dean, John Kerry, Gary Hart, Paul Tsongas, Pat Robertson, and Jerry Brown; nineteen Supreme Court Justices; and several foreign heads of state.

Yale also boasts many state-of-the-art buildings and among the most prized is its "green" medical building at 10 Amistad. Named in honor of the two-masted schooner *La Amistad* (Spanish for "friendship") on which fifty-three West Africans slaves were chained but eventually declared free citizens in a New Haven court in

1841, with the help of Yale-graduate lawyers, 10 Amistad serves as a testament to freedom. It is there that researchers can spend as much time as they need, focused on medical projects that could one day potentially contribute to the health and well-being of people all over the world.

Yale's New Haven location has inextricably linked the town with the gown. Incorporated as a city in 1784, New Haven early on reaped benefits from Yale. In the late eighteenth century, Yale graduate Eli Whitney developed the cotton gin and established a gun-manufacturing factory in New Haven, helping the town to gain a strong manufacturing economy. The Civil War brought an even greater boom to the local economy, with wartime purchases of industrial goods. However, by the 1950s—post–World War II—New Haven, like other U.S. cities, witnessed an industrial decline, as factories closed and workers left town. From the 1960s through the 1990s, New Haven's population continued to nose-dive, as did its economic well-being.

However, during approximately the same time, a positive shift in New Haven's economic base was also slowly taking place. Yale University was expanding, and more and more local residents were being employed by the university. Today, Yale stands as New Haven's largest employer. Fifty-six percent of the city's economy is in the services industry, particularly in education and health care.

But along with the advantageous economic relationship between the university and the residents of the city came an adversarial one, as each group eyed the other warily. Townspeople were angered at the university's expansion, which caused some of its neighborhoods to be razed, resulting in the displacement of longtime residents. Traffic increased on local streets, making it difficult for residents to find parking. And although the university brought with it jobs, many local residents complained that the campus robbed them of tax revenue, as land property was removed from tax rolls. Furthermore, the town was angered by drunkenness tolerated by the notion that "students will be students," as Yalies noisily partied late into the night.

On the other hand, students complained of the violence associated with the town, with drugs, gangs, and homicides an everpresent reality. Differences in economic class and potential, as well as in political and economic views, added to an inevitable underlying distrust, and even disdain, between the two groups.

Efforts on both sides at improving relations have taken place over the years, but however successful, the dichotomy between town and gown still exists—and may never be totally eradicated.

Most Yale students don't have a strong connection to the New Haven community. Particularly at the medical school, where graduates are expected to go on to national leadership roles, students don't stick around for long once they've earned their degrees. Annie Le was one of the best and the brainiest, tapped for a bright future and stellar career.

Now, she would never move on.

THREE

Annie Le, GRD '13 (graduate student scheduled to get her degree in 2013), was among the 11,000 students attending the prestigious university in 2009. In her second year as a Ph.D. candidate in pharmacology at the Yale Medical School, she was excited to be back at school after the summer break, to continue working on the research projects that meant so much to her. As part of an investigative team under faculty adviser Anton Bennett, Le hoped that one day her enzyme research might have a positive effect on such diseases as cancer, diabetes, and muscular dystrophy. Hard-working, dedicated, and diligent, the grad student fervently believed in what she was doing. Since high school, she had been laser-focused on finding a way to help the sick. She *would* make a difference in the lives of people.

On September 8, 2009—the day when Le was first reported missing—a soft breeze gently stirred the green, unfallen leaves on campus. Fall had not yet officially arrived to morph the foliage into the dramatic kaleidoscope of reds, oranges, and yellows that was emblematic of a New England autumn. But the promise of a fresh start was nevertheless in the air. New and returning students scurried from building to building, anxious not to be late to class. Closets filled with pastel T-shirts and belly-revealing shorts were being replaced by plaids of light wool and closed shoes. Backpacks, books, and ballpoints were being whisked off the shelves like candy—or granola bars. A fresh beginning, always a part of a new school year, was in the back of everyone's mind. A good start always portended well.

Le rose early that morning, as usual, eager to go to her lab and check on her mice. After putting on a bright green short-sleeved T-shirt, brown skirt, reddish necklace, and brown mule-type shoes, she left the top-floor apartment in the Victorian building she called home. Located directly east of the Yale campus in the East Rock section of New Haven, the area was known for its majestic red basalt cliffs, its 425-acre park, and its quaint Queen Anne and Victorian architecture. East Rock was considered a gentrified section of New Haven and often referred to as "Grad Haven" because so many Ph.D. candidates lived there. The friendly neighborhood was also home to faculty and staff, as well as local residents.

That morning, Le chose to take Yale Transit—a blue-and-white shuttle bus, with an endearing picture of the Yale mascot, a bulldog, staring out the back window—for the two-mile trip to the Sterling Hall of Medicine. The bus traveled between the campus, the New Haven train stations, and the East Rock neighborhoods. Once in her office, room 225 at 333 Cedar Street, Le planned to do some work before heading out for the three-block walk to her basement research lab at 10 Amistad Street.

After arriving at Sterling, she completed some homework and checked her schedule for the day. Then Le grabbed her magnetic Yale ID card and headed along the quiet streets to Amistad. As usual, so as not to be encumbered at her lab, she left her purse, wallet, and cell phone in her secure office. As was often the case, Le passed only a few people on her way to the lab—down Cedar Street, past Congress and Washington avenues, left on Prince Street, then a right on Amistad—but as always, she smiled as she greeted her fellow students.

Security at the medical school campus—in the Hill neighborhood, about a mile from Yale's main campus—was tight. Only those from the university with valid ID cards could enter the buildings. More than seventy video surveillance cameras were focused on the medical school complex, capturing images of everyone in and around the buildings, as well as those entering and exiting the structures.

One reason for the heightened security was due to the neighborhood. As the medical campus expanded into the Hill area, students were thrust outside the protective ivy walls of the university into an area where poverty and crime were facts of life. But even more importantly, ever since the 1980s, when animal rights activists began breaking into labs, setting free animals and destroying what may have been years of research for scientists, animal research labs at medical schools all over the country had instituted tight security. For Le and other researchers, their Ph.D. theses were based on the experiments they conducted in the labs, and if animal rights activists freed the animals, the years they spent growing cells that could help cancer patients, for example, would be destroyed—and could never be recovered.

At 8:59 a.m., Le swiped her electronic key card and gained entrance to the 120,000-square-foot biomedical research building at 10 Amistad. She then headed down to the lower level toward room G13. As was the case with other rooms in the basement, the door to G13 could not be opened except with a Yale ID card. At exactly 10:11:50 a.m. (exits and entries were recorded down to the second), Le swiped her key card and gained access to G13, the room known as Bennett's lab, which referenced the professor under whose guidance Le and seven other graduate students conducted research. Once inside, she put on a yellow lab coat, walked over to the mouse cages, and began her intense examination of their status. After a few minutes, Le took out her always-present brown leather notebook and began writing up her observations.

It was not unusual for Le to spend many hours each day at her lab, and recently, she hunkered down even longer, hoping to get ahead in her work. On this morning, while she meticulously took notes, her thoughts no doubt wandered to the upcoming weekend. She allowed herself—or rather couldn't help—this "transgression" while in the midst of her research. After all, a girl gets married for the first time only once, and Le's momentous occasion was a mere five days away. She could barely contain her excitement. On Sunday, she and her beloved fiancé, Jon Widawsky, would become man and wife. "Lucky, I'm in love with my best friend :)," she wrote on her Facebook profile.

That Sunday promised to be the best day of her life.

At 12:40 p.m., a fire alarm went off at 10 Amistad—most likely a false alarm, but nevertheless, one to be heeded. From time to time, steam produced by a researcher's experiment tripped the alarm. Everyone who was working inside the building filed out, if not enthusiastically then dutifully, and patiently awaited the all-clear signal to return.

The rest of the afternoon of September 8 held no outward signs of anything untoward taking place at Amistad. Researchers entered their labs, focused on their experiments, and then exited—usually to attend classes or to go to the library to study. Proud professors queried their protégées on the progress they were making. And animal techs signed in on their schedule task sheets, then hurried about, making notes, cleaning cages, and mopping floors.

By day's end, the late summer temperature had climbed to a warm 78° F. The sun shone brightly, and all seemed right with the world.

Le's housemates were not at all concerned when Le had not come home by 4 p.m. or even by 5 p.m. It was often difficult for the studious Le to tear herself away from her research. However, when she hadn't shown up by 7 p.m.—long after her last class of the day—and hadn't phoned her roommate, Natalie Powers, to say where she was, her housemates became concerned. It was unlike Le not to call to tell them of her plans.

Just to make sure everything was copasetic, Powers called Le's cell phone. It rang and rang, and then Le's outgoing message came on. *Perhaps she's studying in the library and turned her phone off,* thought Powers. Just to calm her own nerves, Powers decided to call some of Le's friends and colleagues. One after the next responded that they had not seen or heard from Le since early that morning. Powers hesitated phoning Le's fiancé, who was studying for his Ph.D. at Columbia University in New York City, not wanting to alarm him in case Le was simply studying late somewhere.

But by 9 p.m., Powers was feeling distinctly anxious and decided she had to give Widawsky a call. She tried to keep her voice calm as she asked him if he had been in touch with Le. Widawsky told Powers he hadn't heard from her—very unusual, he said, because during their morning chat at 8 a.m., they had made a plan to speak at 7 p.m. Before hanging up, Powers and Widawsky told each other they would be in touch the second they heard from Le, and then ended their conversation on an uplifting, if perhaps disingenuous note—*I'm sure we'll be hearing from Annie any minute, and she'll be eager to tell us of her unanticipated adventure.*

However, by 10 p.m., with still no word from Le, Powers was unable to calm her worries. After talking the situation over with her housemates, Powers decided to call the Yale Police Department—just to be on the safe side.

While it was not exactly a routine occurrence for the Yale police to receive a missing-person call, it was not exactly out of the ordinary either. They had fielded their share of this type of call before. In the past, they had followed up on many missing persons reports, and in practically every case, the "missing" student turned up casually the next day, simply having done something a little out of the ordinary. If Le was a party girl, for example, she could be somewhere dancing and drinking the night away. If she was the nerdy type, she could be studying late in the library or in a colleague's room. If she liked to surprise people, she could have decided on the spur of the moment to travel home. After all, Le *could* have been anywhere.

The police officer who answered Powers's call asked her to tell him something about Le so the authorities could have a better understanding of the situation. Powers told him of a petite Asian woman, around 4'11" and weighing around 90 pounds, who was studying for her Ph.D. in pharmacology under the tutelage of Anton Bennett. She said that Le had left home that morning to do research in her lab at 10 Amistad and then planned to attend class.

Oh, by the way, Powers added, almost as an after-thought, Le was getting married on Sunday.

Immediately, a red flag went up in the officer's mind. Perhaps Le had gotten cold feet and was rethinking her wedding plans. Maybe she was even following the lead of another recent bride-to-be from Georgia, Jennifer Wilbanks, who had run away before her upcoming wedding and later falsely reported that she had been kidnapped.

The officer tried to calm Powers and assured her that the Yale Police Department would do everything it could to help locate Le. He said that Yale police officers would arrive very shortly at her apartment, 188 Lawrence Street, to delve more deeply into the circumstances. The officer urged Powers to continue making calls to anyone she could think of who might know where Le was and to keep in touch with the police with any news she might have.

Getting right on it, the Yale police went to Le's apartment and spoke with Le's housemates. At the same time, other officers contacted Anton Bennett and relayed Powers's concerns. They asked Le's faculty adviser if he had heard from or seen Le. Bennett responded that Le had been in her office at the Sterling Hall of Medicine earlier in the day, and perhaps they could find some clues as to her whereabouts there.

Not wasting any time, the police headed over to Sterling. The majestic limestone building, built in 1925, had made it possible for Yale to attract a high caliber of faculty, which helped the Yale Medical School attain its present exalted place in medical education. After gaining access to Le's third-floor office, they saw a purse containing a cell phone, credit cards, and cash. Upon further inspection, the police discovered that all the items belonged to Annie Le. *That's odd,* they thought. *Why would someone leave her purse and cell phone behind?* As they looked around the room, they noticed that everything was neat and in its place. There was no forced entry, and nothing obvious was missing. Clearly Le had been in Sterling and then left the office—not in a hurry and seemingly not under duress—to head to her research lab. *Perhaps she didn't want the encumbrance of her purse and the distraction of her phone during the rest of the day.*

Most likely, there was no cause for alarm, as statistics were decidedly in Le's favor. About 2,300 Americans were reported missing each day, but only about 10 percent never returned home.

Surely Annie Le would show up shortly, with a perfectly reasonable story, and the whole incident would be chalked up to yet another false alarm.

Wouldn't it?

FOUR

Tuesday night, September 8, passed achingly slowly for Le's roommate, Natalie Powers, for Le's housemates, but especially for her fiancé, Widawsky, as they waited for any word from Le. Because it was so out of the ordinary for her not to call them to say where she was, they found it hard to keep themselves from thinking dark thoughts. However, they tried to stay optimistic, praying that everything would be cleared up soon—with a happy ending, of course.

As Wednesday morning dawned and Le had neither come home nor called any of her friends or family members, the Yale Police Department began to think that perhaps they were involved in something more alarming than a student gone temporarily AWOL.

Around noon, Le's faculty adviser, Anton Bennett, emailed the pharmacology department chair, Joseph Schlessinger, to report that Le had not shown up for work. Bennett stated he was concerned because Le had failed to notify the other students in his tight-knit eight-person lab team ahead of time that she would be absent—a routine that all the researchers followed.

As the afternoon hours passed and Le missed a pathology class in which she was a teaching assistant, Schlessinger, too, became alarmed, so he notified the dean of the School of Medicine, Robert Alpern, that Le hadn't shown up for class.

By now, word was spreading around campus that Annie Le, Ph.D. candidate, GRD '13, had not been seen since the previous morning. Those who knew Le personally were flabbergasted because it was unheard of for Le not to show up where she was scheduled to be and especially not to show up at her home to sleep. Those who did not know Le personally barely paid any attention to the information. After all, many of them had gone "missing" for a day—spending an overnight and the next day with a new love interest, traveling home without informing anyone ahead of time, or even going on a one-day retreat somewhere—just to get away from all the pressure.

However, as evening's shadows fell and there was still no word from Le, students in hushed voices began to whisper the unthinkable: *Could something criminal have taken place? Could Le have been kidnapped—or worse?* Panic set in as they thought, *What could cause Annie not to call to tell someone where she was?*

Finally, at 7:30 p.m., after Le had not been seen or heard from for more than twenty-four hours, the Yale Police Department put out a statement officially declaring the twenty-four-year-old Le a missing person. It was a defining moment. The police no longer believed it likely that Annie Le was blissfully idling her time away somewhere.

Once the news spread around campus, Deputy University Secretary Martha Highsmith, overseer of campus security operations, attempted to tamp down fears by assuring the community that thus far, there was no evidence of foul play. However, she said, she could not elaborate further because of the now-ongoing investigation. In effect, her words did little to soothe the nerves of the students who, if they gave their imaginations free rein, imagined the worst: *Could Le be dead? Could a killer be loose somewhere?*

The police stepped up their search. They focused on the two places where Le was known to have been the day before. Dozens of police and security officers streamed into Le's office at the Sterling Hall Department of Pharmacology, where they gathered up all of Le's belongings and took them for examination. They combed through 10 Amistad and the attached parking garage, hoping to find a clue as to where Le might be. They raked through garbage bins outside the building, and they collected the footage from the seventy-plus surveillance cameras that dotted the area around Amistad.

Some of the police hunkered down to scrutinize the videos. Slowly and painstakingly, they viewed every single image on the grainy film. Within a short time, they came upon a clear image of Le entering 10 Amistad on Tuesday, September 8, wearing a green T-shirt and carrying an unidentified object. However, as thoroughly as they examined the pictures, they could not find an image of Le leaving the building—even during the fire alarm that cleared Amistad at 12:40 p.m.

Of course, it was possible that the police were not able to locate the petite Le in the surveillance video if, while everyone was exiting the building, Le was obscured by bigger and taller people or if she had put on a sweater or coat and looked altogether different. But nevertheless, with no image of Le leaving Amistad—either during the fire drill or at any other time during the day—the police were becoming concerned.

In the evening, after the authorities searched both Sterling and Amistad, university vice president and secretary Linda Lorimer told the Yale community and the press, "We have been looking now at all of the tapes of every exit and entrance [of 10 Amistad] over the entire twenty-four hours, just to see if there's any information we can give to the law enforcement agencies." But unfortunately, she said, they did not find a single clue.

Martha Highsmith reiterated that there was still no evidence to suggest foul play, but she reported that the university had decided to be proactive and call in the New Haven Police, the Connecticut State Police, and the Federal Bureau of Investigation to assist the Yale Police Department in the search for Le.

Bringing in the big guns only increased the alarm that everyone involved was feeling.

The Yale Police Department distributed the surveillance photo showing Le entering 10 Amistad on Tuesday morning, along with a leaflet, which stated that Le left her purse, credit cards, and cash at her Sterling office on Tuesday. It went on to say what she was wearing; that she had no access to a car; and that she didn't have any apparent medical conditions that would help explain her disappearance. It asked that anyone with information about Le's whereabouts contact the Yale Police Department at 203-432-4400.

At day's end, Le's co-worker Debbie Apuzzo remarked, "She left her pocketbook, cell phone in the lab. She didn't go home last night. She is getting married on Sunday. Her fiancé hasn't heard from her. Everybody is pretty worried, pretty scared."

Le's adviser Bennett dittoed the sentiment. "The biggest thing we're worried about right now is 'Is she okay?'"

FIVE

Where was Annie Le, and was she okay? This was the question on everyone's mind at Yale. But the police agencies now involved in the search had still another question: *Who* was Annie Le? Maybe if they knew more about her—her background, her personality and habits, who she hung out with—they'd find some scrap of knowledge to help locate her.

Annie Le hailed from Placerville, California, a city of around 10,000 people located in the foothills of the scenic Sierra Nevada. Placerville was originally known as "Dry Diggins," after the way in which California gold miners in the 1840s carried the dry soil to water to separate it from gold. Later, the city was called "Hangtown," because of its many public hangings of murderers of miners, who had "unfortunately" come upon the much-coveted gold. But Placerville of the twenty-first century was a far cry from its rowdy Gold Rush beginnings. Charming and historic, Placerville was considered an ideal place in which to settle down and raise a family.

Le felt lucky to have grown up there. Born on July 3, 1985, in San Jose to Vietnamese parents Hoang and Vivian Van Le, who were now divorced (Hoang was remarried), Le was raised by her aunt and uncle,

Ngoc-Tuyet Bui and Robert Linh Nguyen. First-generation Americans, Le and her brother Chris Le grew up in modest circumstances with their "guardian parents" and the Buis' three children in a remote ranch-style home, deep in the woods off a winding, one-lane gravel road. Miles from the nearest town, it was rural, rustic, and picturesque—an idyllic place for the youngsters to play and explore.

Le attended Union Mine High School, around forty-five miles east of Sacramento. While there, she was accepted as a member of the National Honor Society, a noteworthy nationwide organization that recognizes excellence in scholarship, leadership, service, and character. In her class of 362 people, Le was awarded the prestigious title of valedictorian, with a 4.28 grade point average. Well-liked and extremely smart, her classmates voted her "Best of the Best," as well as the female student "Most Likely to be the Next Einstein." In the yearbook picture showing the two likely Einsteins (Le and a male student), Le is smiling broadly, wearing a white lab coat. The partially dissected cat in her arms vied with her happy face for attention.

In her valedictory speech, Le told the teachers, students, and parents about her plans for the future. She said she loved cell biology and figuring out how things worked on a microscopic level. She stated that her goal was to become a "laboratory pathologist—it's one step above surgery." Then, with her customary humor, she wrote in her senior yearbook, "So, I've got to go to school for about twelve years first and get my MD and be certified as a surgeon. I just hope that all that hard work is going to pay off and I'm really going to enjoy my job."

During her senior year of high school, while working as a volunteer at Marshall Medical Center in El

Dorado County, Le was named Volunteer of the Year for the 2002–03 academic year. Her supervisor, Dr. Gary Martin, director of operations in the center's pathology department, said, "We used to joke that she could do a calculus problem quicker than she could wash a bottle." Yet, he continued, she would bottle-wash happily. After she completed her "mundane chores," he said, she would sit next to a pathologist and look at a slide through a microscope, and soak in the knowledge. Martin remarked that Le was the best student he ever had as a volunteer. Calling her "a little stick of dynamite," he said she was "smart, she was vivacious, always cheery, a ton of energy."

Kathleen Gleason, who worked with the hospital volunteers while Le volunteered at the center, said, "You couldn't help but love her. At her young age, how confident she was. Not all kids at that age are that smart and driven and have friends. She seemed to have it all." In a show of gratitude for her outstanding work, the medical center awarded her a $500 scholarship toward college.

Teachers at Union Mine High School also felt that Le stood out, calling her "intelligent" and "confident." They said she had a passion for science and knew exactly where she wanted to go and what she wanted to do. Principal Tony DeVille called her "one of the brightest spots in the school's history." Students, too, felt she was special. They considered her friendly, upbeat, and spunky— and so brilliant.

In spite of all the acclaim she received throughout her high school years, Le wasn't being handed her future on a silver platter. She filled out 102 applications for college scholarships—hopeful that at least *one* place would see fit to award her a sum of money so she could pursue her career dreams. "My tongue is sore from licking envelopes, my wrist hurts from typing and stapling, and the post office clerk knows me on a first name basis," she wrote in a one-page note she left in the files of her high school, "but other than that, there is nothing I can complain about. It was not difficult at all!"

After carefully scrutinizing the pros and cons of dozens of universities and colleges, Le decided that Princeton University, on the opposite side of the country in New Jersey, was her first choice. It seemed to offer everything she wanted. Princeton was world-renowned, "distinctive among research universities in its commitment to undergraduate teaching." And research was exactly what Le wanted to do.

So in the spring of 2003, Le applied to Princeton and anxiously waited for a thick bundle to show up in the mailbox, signaling acceptance. However, that was not to be. Princeton turned her down. Although she was heartbroken, she managed to find some humor in the situation. According to Cierra Silva Montes, a high school classmate of Le's, Le sent a photograph of her derriere to the dean of admissions. *That will show them!* laughed Le. Montes called her a "spunky little thing," who had not only book smarts, but street smarts as well.

Le received many college acceptances and after weighing her options, decided that the University of Rochester—which offered her $160,000 in scholarship money—was the place she wanted to go. In September 2003, Le headed three thousand miles east to the cold climes of northern New York State, where snowfall averaged around a hundred inches a year—in contrast to the dusting-to-six-inches that might occur in Placerville. Considered one of the premier research universities in the country, Rochester prided itself on its low student-to-teacher ratio and its highly accomplished teaching staff. According to one former student, the University of Rochester curriculum was incredible: "There was a ton of freedom in selecting the courses you wanted to take, rather than fulfilling random core requirements." Although the city of Rochester was a far cry from Placerville in distance, weather, and lifestyle, it was nevertheless a delightful place to attend college. Located on the Erie Canal, only five miles south of Lake Ontario, Rochester was named one of the top ten most livable cities in America in 2007, the year Le graduated. Aside from the many winter sports Rochester afforded, the warmer months offered hiking, sailing and canoeing, camping, and exploring in over two thousand acres of parklands.

At Rochester, Le's research centered on the genetics of speciation (the evolution of one of more species from an existing species), using Nasonia, a parasitic wasp, as a model, but she was also involved in other research projects. The National Institutes of Health, one of the world's foremost medical research centers, recognized Le's achievements in investigating the molecular basis of osteoarthritis by awarding her a fellowship to work at the Institute in Bethesda, Maryland, for the summers of 2005 and 2006. The "Meet the Scholars" website of the NIH declared that the undergraduate scholarship program "offers competitive scholarships to exceptional students from disadvantaged backgrounds who are committed to biomedical, behavioral, and social science research careers at the NIH."

Although still an undergraduate, having just completed her sophomore year, Le headed south, eager to soak up the knowledge and experience the NIH offered. Once there, she made good friends and gained invaluable knowledge, which she later applied to her Yale research. According to a biography on the NIH website,

Le conducted a project on bone tissue engineering, using mouse mesenchymal stem cells, which are cells that can develop into a variety of different things, from connective and supporting tissue to smooth muscle and blood cells. The purpose of the project, said Le, was to further understand the process of bone formation in order "to manipulate it and regenerate bone tissue in patients suffering from degenerative bone diseases." In her self-profile for the NIH, she wrote that although she enjoyed her biology studies, she wanted to pursue research in medical anthropology, "which has highlighted the severity of health issues in societies worldwide."

While attending Rochester, Le still managed to find time to volunteer at a soup kitchen and also attend church—and to pursue an abiding passion besides science: shopping. Le would shop for bargains any chance she got, coveting items from $2 T-shirts to vintage Chanel clothing—at under $5. A quirky dresser, Le would often wear very high heels, and their click-click-click in the halls signaled that Le was about to arrive at class. She loved big, dangling earrings and clingy dresses. Although brilliant, she was not at all nerdy.

Le's physics professor, Steven Manly, called Le a star. "Always would leave a smile on your face, good-humored, and beautiful." Le's lab partner in physics class, Brad Grattan, commented that Le was "always very focused on what she was doing."

After four grueling but invigorating and enriching years at the University of Rochester, Le graduated in 2007 with honors with a major in cell and developmental biology and a minor in medical anthropology. Le received an award from the biology department for her academic achievements, as well as a college leadership award. As she had proven in the past, Le took her academic life seriously and was determined to excel.

But academic pursuits—and shopping—were not all that Le focused on at Rochester. While attending the university, she met Jonathan Widawsky, a fellow student from Huntington, New York. At first, the two were just friends who had many interests in common. But in time, their friendship blossomed into romance, and the two kindred souls fell deeply in love.

Although it wasn't an easy decision to make, when it came time to graduate from Rochester, Le and Widawsky decided to go their separate ways to get their Ph.D.'s—Le to Yale and Widawsky to Columbia, where he would pursue a degree in applied physics and mathematics. They highly respected each other's work and were determined not to put pressure on each other to sacrifice their goals for the relationship. However, they promised each other that they would do whatever it took to stay in touch daily and to visit each other by making the hour-and-a-half trip between campuses as often as possible. They vowed to keep their relationship alive. Although miles separated them, in their hearts, they knew they would always be right next to each other.

Le entered Yale in September 2007, a doctoral student in the class of '13 at the School of Medicine's Department of Pharmacology. As her first school term progressed, she began to hone in on the research that meant most to her: how certain types of fatty acids regulate an enzyme involved in preventing metabolic disorders and in treating cancer and other diseases. As part of Anton Bennett's laboratory, Le was also involved in several other cutting-edge research projects.

During her second year as a grad student, Le chose her dissertation topic: the effects of certain proteins on metabolic diseases, such as diabetes. One way she researched her topic was by doing experiments on mice, which meant she was often in the basement lab of 10

Amistad, where the mice were housed. That year, Le also received a grant from the National Science Foundation, an independent federal agency that promoted, among other things, the progress of science and the advance of national health. At the end of her second year as a Ph.D. candidate, as she continued to excel in graduate school and to work hard on the research that meant so much to her, she found time to pay attention to something else that meant the world to her—a wedding.

In July 2008, Le and Widawsky got engaged and made the all-important decision to get married the following year. The decision came without any doubts. They could not imagine being with anyone else for the rest of their lives. Widawsky proposed to Le after they spent a day walking in the park, having a "chocolate dinner," and going to a good friend's birthday party. They planned a honeymoon in Greece.

The couple chose Sunday, September 13, 2009, as their wedding day and decided on an 11 a.m. ceremony at a gazebo overlooking a pond at the North Ritz Club in Syosset, New York—close to Widawsky's childhood home. According to the Ritz Club's website, the club "unites our expertise with your inspiration."

And Le and Widawsky had plenty of inspiration. Following the service, the 160 invited guests would be treated to an open bar and an early afternoon meal. According to Nadeen Fotopoulos, manager in charge of the banquet, Le had chosen every food item and was "very excited to get married." A friend of Le's, Jennifer Simpson, said that Le had even planned the details of table napkins and flowers. Of course, there would be plenty of toasts and lots of dancing. Le regularly checked on weather patterns, hoping that the day of her wedding would be sunny and warm. On a May 13 posting to

Le's wedding blog, Le wrote: "In terms of consumables, I'm most excited about the pigs-in-the-blanket." And on September 6, Le wrote on her Facebook page, "Less than one week til the big day!"

Le hired Deborah Kiley, of Deborah's Hairloft in Huntington, to do her hair and makeup on the morning of the wedding. The bride-to-be had decided on a "slick back bun and very simple makeup." Le planned to have a manicure and pedicure on Friday, two days before the wedding. "She wanted everything perfect," said Kiley.

Le and Widawsky had something of a dress rehearsal in the summer of 2009, when, in a gesture to those who lived too far away to attend the East Coast wedding, the couple flew to Santa Ana, California and, decked out in their wedding attire—including a stunning veil that Le had painstakingly embroidered—held a reception for family and friends. According to those who attended, it was a festive and magical occasion, and Le beamed as she spent time with relatives, proudly showing off her husband-to-be.

To preside over the wedding ceremony, the couple had chosen Cantor Sandra Sherry of Temple Beth El in Huntington, Long Island, who had known Widawsky since he was a baby. In that role, Sherry always spoke to the prospective brides and grooms before their wedding and asked them why they want to be married. "Annie clearly said Jonathan brought out the best in her and that she's very in love with him," said Sherry. "They reached a level of maturity that said they were ready for matrimony." Widawsky was happiest when he was around Annie. And the feeling was reciprocated. Le's smile, said the cantor, "was effervescent when she spoke about the wedding."

As the wedding day approached, Le was feeling totally comfortable about having a Jewish wedding ceremony. After all, she had been studying Hebrew for several months and was feeling confident in her ability to understand the service.

Le and Widawsky had signed up for a gift registry on WeddingChannel.com. They picked a store, Macy's, and selected silverware, bed linens, towels, a sewing machine, vacuum cleaner, and even a "colorful gravy boat." They also selected a charity from a list of over a hundred compiled by WeddingChannel. It was the "I Have a Dream" Foundation, which seemed a perfect match for their interest in education. The charity was dedicated to helping low-income children pursue higher education by providing them with the skills and knowledge they needed to go on to college. A national organization, the "I Have a Dream" Foundation stayed with the children from elementary school until they completed high school and then guaranteed tuition support for college. The couple also chose a second foundation, "I Do," a Washington, D.C.–based group that linked engaged couples to charities.

"They're so young and they're starting out doing philanthropy," stated the managing editor of Wedding Channel.com. "That they wished to start out by giving back to others says a lot about them."

So with their summer reception behind them and their nerves a bit more under control, Le and Widawsky couldn't wait for their big day, knowing they would be able to thoroughly enjoy it. Le said she would be spending the rest of her life with "the person I love most in life."

So on Tuesday, September 8, with so much still left to do and with so little time in which to do it, Le focused even more intently on her animal research in the basement of 10 Amistad. She was so excited and so much in love—and was joyfully counting down the days.

Only five to go!

SIX

Although Le had now been missing for over twenty-four hours, those closest to her felt oddly calmed by one fact. In February, Le had written an article titled "Crime and Safety in New Haven," which appeared in the School of Medicine's *B Magazine,* a student publication of the School of Medicine's Combined Program in the Biological and Biomedical Sciences.

The article began with a brief background of Yale, stating that it was a large community, consisting of over 11,000 students and approximately the same number of faculty and staff, and that it was "protected by a full-service police force that works in conjunction with the City of New Haven."

However, Le wrote, in spite of such safety measures as shuttle services and door-to-door escorts, on-campus thefts were on the increase. Some of those thefts, she reported, involved "frightening confrontation." Comparing on-campus motor thefts from 2005 to those in 2007, Le stated the number of thefts had doubled: 167 "events" were recorded in 2007. Le then compared this number to that which took place at other universities: nearby Quinnipiac University had at most two thefts per year; Southern Connecticut University, also in New

Haven but farther from the downtown area, had ten thefts on its campus in 2007.

Le then cited Columbia University's Morningside and Medical Center campuses, a city college like Yale, stating that it had approximately the same number of auto thefts as Yale—168—but Columbia had twice as many enrolled students. The University of Pennsylvania, Le cited, also with over 22,000 students, reported only fifty-three thefts. Harvard's Cambridge and Longwood campuses, with 26,000 students, reported 324 thefts. "As it stands," Le wrote, "Yale experiences more thefts per student than any of these metropolitan Ivy League Institutions."

Le also reported that according to CNN's *Money* magazine, the city of New Haven had "7 times as much personal crime compared to the average for 'safe' cities in the United States."

For the article, Le interviewed the chief of the Yale Police Department, James Perrotti, who offered several pointers on how students could remain safe:

1. Pay attention to where you are.
2. Avoid portraying yourself as a potential victim.
3. Do not be distracted by iPods and phone calls.
4. Reduce your exposure (use the Yale escort and shuttle services).
5. Walk with a purpose.
6. Keep a minimum amount on your person.

Le ended her article by presenting this warning: "New Haven is a city, and all cities have their perils, but with a little street smarts, one can avoid becoming yet another statistic."

Obviously, Le had thought a great deal about safety in New Haven, and had tried to alert others to possible dangers. She had even taken her own advice to heart. "She doesn't walk around at night by herself," Le's friend Jennifer Simpson told reporters. "If she had to work late, she would make sure someone could come pick her up or walk with her."

Now, one could only pray that her forethought and insights were enough to have kept her safe.

SEVEN

Although the disappearance of Annie Le was certainly an aberration in the daily life at Yale, the university's history, which included nearly every accolade an institution of higher learning could receive, was nevertheless not without its dark side. And Le herself was acutely aware that Yale—despite its Ivy-hood—was not always the safest of places. Notably, the university had accumulated its share of bizarre and sensational crimes. A professor in the department of computer science had nearly had his hand blown off by a mail bomb sent by Theodore Kaczynski, the infamous Unabomber. When Hollywood actress Jodie Foster attended Yale, she was stalked by an obsessed fan, John W. Hinkley Jr., who not long after—in a claimed attempt to earn Foster's "respect and love"—tried to assassinate President Ronald Reagan. And in 2003, an explosive device was set off in the Sterling Law Building—just hours after finals and less than twenty-four hours after the Department of Homeland Security under President George W. Bush had raised the nation's terror alert level to orange—the second highest level of alert. No one was injured in the law building blast, but two classrooms were seriously damaged. And the perpetrator was never caught.

By the same token, Yale has had its share of what

the police might consider more "mundane" crimes, the types of law-breaking that resulted from juxtaposing a rich institution like Yale against a relatively impoverished neighborhood like the one abutting the campus: muggings, robberies—the types of wrongdoing that Annie Le wrote about in her article. Although in recent years, the neighborhoods surrounding Yale have improved and even prospered somewhat, street crime continues and Yale students are sometimes the targets.

Compared to today, the crime rates at Yale and in surrounding New Haven were almost intolerable in the '80s and early '90s, triggered initially by the city of New Haven's virtual economic collapse. Starting in the 1950s, New Haven began to experience an economic downturn due to the exodus of middle-class workers. In the 1960s and 1970s, the city, like many manufacturing cities in New England, suffered a severe economic depression. Manufacturers were relocating, the population was declining, factories were closing, and many people were out of work. In fact, the city's population fell by more than a quarter, to 122,000 residents. About 50,000 of those who remained in the city were poor, unskilled, undereducated, or unemployed—and often all of these. More than 20 percent of the city lived below the poverty line. Poverty and violent crime increased over the next four decades, as New Haven continued to decline in population and prosperity. Even today, poverty and crime remain a problem in some central neighborhoods, causing many to call the city "gritty," "grimy," and worse.

The stark contrast between many of the residents of New Haven and the students attending Yale was not lost on anyone living in the area. The great divide— between that of mostly privileged, preppy, rich, white kids and impoverished, unskilled, undereducated, and unemployed blacks—was thrust onto the national stage whenever a major criminal incident occurred involving a student. Then, the media would pick up the situation, blast it over the airwaves, and university personnel, politicians, and residents alike would talk seriously about safety conditions on urban campuses all over the country, as well as on the specific relationship Yale had with its own home city.

Two frightening crimes in particular continue to stand out—burned indelibly into the collective Yale memory.

In 1990, a test given in the schools of New Haven's poorest districts showed that fewer than a tenth of the students read at or above grade level. Although heroin had been a staple in the city since the 1960s, by 1990, cocaine trafficking had made significant inroads and soon became an even bigger crisis. Distribution of the drug brought with it the inevitable gangs, and with the gangs came the inevitable gang rivalry and related violence. Turf wars took place as rival gangs staked out their territory. Drive-by shootings in broad daylight became a fact of life in the city. Between 1989 and 1991, 1,162 shootings—more than one per day—took place in New Haven, half of them as a result of gang violence.

Even with the ominous situation in New Haven, many believed that an iron curtain, heavily laced with ivy, kept the disparate worlds of Yale privilege and New Haven squalor from intersecting.

However, the iron curtain soon proved to be as flimsy as a leaf on February 17, 1991. On that day, Christian Haley Prince, class of '93 and a fourth-generation Yalie, had eaten dinner at Mory's, a private club open to only those who are affiliated with Yale, and then attended a party at the Aurelian Senior Society at Yale's sandstone Sterling-Sheffield-Strathcona Hall. After the festivities, most of Prince's friends continued the good time and headed to the popular Naples pizzeria. But Prince wanted to get to bed "early" so he could be at his best for lacrosse practice the next day. So at 1 a.m., the nineteen-year-old, 6'2" blond, blue-eyed sophomore began the five-minute stroll to his off-campus apartment, at the corner of Whitney Avenue and Trumbull Streets. Heading down Hillhouse Avenue, even in the dark of night, he was awestruck as always by the grandeur of the majestic boulevard that, according to tradition, both Charles Dickens and Mark Twain called the "most beautiful street in all America." Grand home after grand home lined the avenue—the Mary Pritchard two-story, three-bay-wide stuccoed brick Greek Revival; the Elizabeth Apthorp House, with its bracketed overhanging eaves and window hoods; the Aaron N. Skinner House, with its Ionic order portico; the Graves-Dwight House, with its classic detailing; the John P. Norton House, with a projecting four-story front tower; and on and on—all fronted by enormous elms and evergreens.

As Prince turned left onto Hillhouse Avenue, he stared up at the impressive Gothic Revival style edifice that was St. Mary's Church, the oldest Catholic parish in New Haven, established in 1832. Only one block from the official residence of Yale president, Benno C. Schmidt Jr., Prince no doubt felt secure in the vicinity of the impressive community of scholars of which he was proud to be a part.

At 1:15 a.m., a graduate student on her way to the Yale Health Center at 17 Hillhouse Avenue saw what she thought was a body splayed in front of the middle steps of the church. Although she believed that seeing

an actual dead body in front of the church was about
as likely as witnessing a miracle, she nevertheless felt
she should check it out. As she neared the form, there,
in front of the church in New Haven's most privileged
neighborhood, was the lifeless body of a white male, a
bullet hole in the center of his overcoat. Immediately
she contacted the police. In less than an hour, at 2:05
a.m., Sunday, February 17, 1991, Christian Prince was
declared dead at Yale-New Haven Hospital.

Three months later, in May, police arrested sixteen-
year-old James Duncan Fleming, known as Dunc, a black
youth from a poor family in the Newhallville neighborhood of New Haven. A member of two gangs—the
Lynch Mob and Ville gangs—Dunc was fingered by
Randy Fleming (no relation). According to Randy Fleming's original statement, he and Dunc needed money
for a rap concert, and Dunc suggested they "stick up a
cracker." As they were driving along, they saw the
perfect target in a lone "cracker" on Hillhouse Avenue.
Dunc stopped the car, walked up to Prince with his pis-
tol prominently displayed, and demanded Prince's cash.
Prince immediately handed over his wallet. According to Fleming, Dunc then said, "I ought to shoot this
cracker," and with that, after first striking him with the
gun, Dunc fired a shot into Prince's chest.

Four charges were leveled against Dunc: first-degree
murder; felony murder; attempted robbery; and conspiracy. A trial date was set. On the stand, Randy Fleming recanted his statements, stating that the police had
coerced him into lying. So with no witnesses and no
firsthand accounts, it proved impossible to convict Dunc
of first-degree murder. The jury, however, was deadlocked on the felony murder (death that occurs in the
commission or attempted commission of a felony) and
attempted robbery charges, but convicted Dunc of the

charge of conspiracy to rob. For that, he was given a nine-year sentence.

A new trial date was set for March 1993 to try Dunc on the two deadlocked charges. After the trial and jury deliberations, this second jury acquitted James Duncan Fleming on the two outstanding charges.

After the trial, Edward Prince, the dead man's father, said, "I felt that the jury deeply hurt us with their decision." Later, the slain man's mother said she believed the tragedy was not only for her family, but for the Flemings as well. They struggled to raise their child in a gun-filled, drug-filled, violence-ridden neighborhood, she said. "We are so terribly aware that these children have no chance in life."

Prince's death prompted a book, *Dead Opposite: The Lives and Loss of Two American Boys,* by Geoffrey Douglas, along with countless articles about the vast divide between gown and town. In his book, Douglas exposed the ever-widening gap between whites and blacks and came to the conclusion that there are, indeed, two societies in America, which are "not at war, not separate but totally estranged."

After the Prince murder, applications to Yale for the 1991–92 school year dropped 9.5 percent.

On the tenth anniversary of Christian Prince's death, in February 2001, an article in the *Yale Daily News* included this sentiment:

"For Yale, the Prince murder represented not just an isolated tragedy but a failure, possibly unavoidable, to keep its students safe. It was a painful reminder that even the heart of the University's campus cannot be a crime-free refuge in an urban environment."

In time, Prince's killing became known as "the murder that changed it all." After Prince's death, Yale began to pay more attention to security and to the gulf that

separated the ivied walls of Yale from the bleakness
that was New Haven. Yale began to beef up its security.
It increased police funding and installed a network of
blue phones and better lighting to help ensure the safety
of the Yale community. It added bike patrols and created
a new security force. And perhaps more importantly,
Yale began an outreach program to the inexorably inter-
twined New Haven community.

But would that be enough to stop bad things from
happening?

By 1998, it had been almost seven years since Prince
was murdered, and the crime rate in New Haven had
dropped by more than 30 percent. Yale seemed safer
than it had been in years—and getting even safer. But
that feeling of security didn't last for long.

Suzanne Jovin, Yale class of '99, was a popular student and a person the university was proud of. She was
a volunteer tutor at the Yale Tutoring In Elementary
Schools program. She co-founded the German club. She
worked in the Davenport dining hall, and she sang in
both the Freshman Chorus and the Bach Society Or-
chestra.

A native of Goettingen, Germany, Jovin had spent
the past three and a half inspiring years at Yale, an honor
she never let herself forget, and as a senior, she had
mixed feelings about graduating and leaving behind
the place she loved so much.

At 4:15 p.m. on December 4, 1998, Jovin dropped
off the penultimate draft of her senior thesis on Osama
bin Laden. No doubt, she felt a great sense of liberation.
Finally, after working so hard, she was nearing the finish line.

Relieved, Jovin spent the early part of the evening at
a holiday pizza party for Best Buddies at New Haven's

Trinity Lutheran Church, an organization that paired students with adults suffering from intellectual disabilities. After the party, Jovin stayed to help clean up, and at 8:30 p.m., she drove another volunteer home in a borrowed university station wagon. At around 8:45 p.m., she dropped off the car at the Yale lot on the corner of Edgewood Avenue and Howe Street and began the two-block walk to her apartment, on the second floor of 258 Park Street.

Several of her friends saw her at her apartment at 8:50 p.m., after she parked the borrowed car. At around 9:25 p.m., she passed Peter Stein '99 on Elm Street and told him she was returning the keys to the car to the Yale police communications center under the arch at Phelps Gate on Yale's Old Campus. At around 9:30 p.m., she was seen again, walking northeast on College Street, by a student returning from a hockey game. The two did not chat.

At 9:55 p.m., a passerby dialed 911 to report a woman bleeding at the corner of Edgehill Avenue and East Rock Road. She reported that the person was fully clothed, on her stomach, with her body on the grassy patch between the road and the sidewalk, and her feet dangling into the street.

Within minutes, the police arrived—to find the dead body of a young co-ed, her throat slit and her head and neck stabbed seventeen times. Jovin was only 1.9 miles from central campus, in New Haven's wealthy East Rock neighborhood. Police found cash in her pocket and a watch on her wrist. It did not appear that she had been robbed or sexually assaulted. And given the time frame, police believed Jovin had been driven to the location where her body was discovered.

Witnesses said they heard a man and a woman arguing on East Rock Road about ten minutes before the

911 call was made—and that the argument had escalated. An examination of Jovin's extensive wounds showed she had been attacked from behind, perhaps as she was walking away from whomever she had been arguing with. No weapon was ultimately found, but the tip of a steel blade was discovered embedded in the back of her skull.

Immediately after the crime, Jovin's thesis adviser and lecturer in the political science department, James Van de Velde, class of '82, became the leading suspect. The police interrogated him for hours, shoving photos of Jovin's dead body under his nose. The next day the *New Haven Register* had a screaming headline, "Yale Teacher Grilled in Killing," and Van de Velde was assailed by television crews. Although he was never charged and no evidence was ever presented against him, he was fired from Yale and remained under a dark cloud for many years. In 2000, after DNA from under Jovin's nails was analyzed, Van de Velde was finally dismissed as a suspect. However, the damage to his career and reputation—not to mention his psyche—had been done.

The Yale Police Department came under attack for the sloppy way they handled the investigation. Cited among its errors were the fact that they refused the help of a state forensic team and other law enforcement agencies; they never submitted a Fresca bottle that was found at the crime scene for DNA testing; and their tunnel vision, which caused them to focus solely on Van de Velde as the perpetrator, lacked any credibility and thwarted investigation into other possible suspects.

To this day, the murderer of Suzanne Jovin has never been found. But because of the viciousness of the crime—without rape or theft as a motive—and because Jovin was believed to have voluntarily been driven to the tony, tree-lined neighborhood where she was killed, investigators continue to believe her attacker was someone she knew.

Had something like one of these incidents happened to Le? Had she been attacked on the street like Prince and become the victim of a robbery that escalated into something worse? If so, where was her body? And why was there no record of her leaving her Amistad lab on any of the surveillance tapes?

Or perhaps Le had been specifically targeted like Jovin was thought to have been. Would she end up like Jovin—with no one knowing what had happened to her? To her friends and loved ones, it felt like Le had vanished off the face of the earth. Among the wider population of Yale students and faculty, the legacy of Prince's and Jovin's murders hung like a shroud over the investigation into Le's disappearance.

And now, as of September 10, 2009, Annie Le had been missing for two entire days. Everyone still held out hope that she would be found, that the whole incident would turn out to be some misunderstanding, that she had slipped away to do some last-minute wedding planning. But lurking in the back of every well-wisher's mind was also the nagging worry that Le's story would end badly— that hers would become another sinister tale in Yale's hallowed history.

EIGHT

As if all that was going on with the investigation of Le's disappearance wasn't enough for the Yale community to deal with, at 9:02 a.m. on Thursday morning, September 10, a man arrived on campus looking for the Human Resources Department. A Yale employee told him that the office had been moved and directed him to the new address. However, because the "visitor" looked suspicious and carried a suspicious-looking package, the employee called the Yale Police Department on a campus blue phone. Only a minute later, the authorities rushed in and apprehended the man in a parking lot near the Human Resources Department.

As it turned out, John Petrini, sixty-one, was carrying an unloaded gun, along with plenty of ammunition. He seemed determined to settle a score he had had with the university. Petrini told the police that he was an ex-Yale employee who had been denied an appeal the previous year, after the university refused to grant him retirement benefits. He stated that his appeal was turned down because when he left the university in 2002, he had not yet reached the minimum age requirement of fifty-five in order to receive benefits.

The Yale Police immediately placed him under arrest.

Interviewed after the incident, the police stated that they felt Petrini may have been targeting the staff inside the Human Resources building—and had he succeeded, the toll in lives lost could have been alarming.

The Yale community was told of the incident in an email message from Yale police chief James Perrotti at 1:33 p.m. Thursday. So, with one positive ending to an incident on the Yale campus, could it be too much to hope for a second? Certainly, the entire Yale community prayed it was not.

Although it was sunny and bright on Thursday morning, spirits around campus didn't match the weather. There was still no word from Annie Le, and people began not only to fear the worst, but to fear for their own lives as well.

Chief Perrotti sent an email to the Yale community, urging anyone with information about the missing student to immediately contact his office. He stated that the authorities had held off sending out the email because the police "do get reports of missing persons, and most of the time, through our investigation, we are able to figure out where the person is." However, because Annie Le had not been seen or heard from for more than forty-eight hours, the police, as well as anyone else who was aware of what was going on, knew that the situation was serious—if not dire.

Many of Le's friends, colleagues, professors, and even her fiancé, who had come to New Haven from New York, joined the more than one hundred law enforcement officials from the various agencies in the search. Widawsky told his roommate at Columbia, Dory Kramer, "They don't know where Annie is. I better go." Kramer commented that Widawsky was distraught. According to Yale University vice president and secretary Linda

Lorimer, Le's fiancé, Widawsky, was cooperating with law enforcement officials and "there's not a worry about his possible involvement in the disappearance." Widawsky, however, did not speak to the media.

At around 1 p.m., four FBI agents showed up at Le's apartment at 188 Lawrence Street. They proceeded up to the third floor, where Le lived, and for over two hours, rifled through the grad student's belongings. By 3:39 p.m., after having been joined by six more agents, they exited her home with a bagful of belongings. The agents did not reveal what the bag contained.

By now, a missing person flier, showing both Le's face, with large circular earrings, and a still photo from the security camera of Le entering 10 Amistad, was being distributed all over the campus—on trees, lampposts, benches, and inside all the dorms and classroom buildings. Electronic billboards on Interstates 91 and 95 displayed the full-face photo of Le, with a large hoop earring dangling from her right ear, asking motorists with information to contact the FBI. The billboard read:

MISSING PERSON
ANNIE LE

Asian Female   Age 24   4'11"   90 pounds
Missing from Amistad Street New Haven

Last Seen: Wearing Bright Green T-Shirt & Brown Skirt
Contact TIPS line at 877-503-1950

In the early hours of the investigation, after Le was first reported missing late on September 8, police did not focus their attention on any one particular place as the possible location of a crime. That's because they weren't at all certain that a crime had, in fact, been committed—or if Le had voluntarily disappeared. But as the days wore on, investigators had become increasingly more convinced that they were dealing with something more ominous than a missing-person case, and they turned their attention to the Amistad lab, where Le was last seen, and to everyone who worked there. The authorities were working on the assumption that if something criminal occurred, the perpetrator must have been a person with a Yale ID card because no one without that card could enter Amistad. The officials were specifically focusing on those students and employees who entered Amistad on September 8.

By midafternoon of September 10, still without suspects or any evidence of foul play, the police revved up their search. Using blueprints of the building, the authorities began inspecting all the rooms and hallways of Amistad. Specific officers were stationed inside each room, while others were positioned at various locations along the halls. Because the area was not officially a crime scene, the building remained open to researchers, staff members, and animal techs, who carried on doing their jobs. "K9s," trained scent-tracking dogs, were brought in as well, but many of the sniffer dogs seemed confused by the different animal smells in the building.

By nightfall, Le's brother and her aunt and uncle flew to New Haven to be close to the situation and to help in any way they could.

Close to tears, Le's faculty adviser Anton Bennett spoke to the media. He said that Le was part of his family. "We are just concerned. We are like her parents."

By day's end, Yale officials still did not have any answers about where Annie Le was, although Linda Lorimer stated, "We are responding to this at this point as if it could be any kind of bad situation. You don't just not go home for a couple of days."

University president Richard Levin took a less ominous position. He stated that, although Yale students had gone missing previously, "fortunately it has in most cases turned out to be a student simply voluntarily leaving without giving notice to people. Every time it happens, we take it with the utmost seriousness." In an effort to quell growing fears among the students and faculty that a murderer might be in their midst, Levin added that the tight security at Amistad had allowed the police to focus in on a few key individuals and that those people were being closely monitored. Plus, Levin stated, the FBI has set up a twenty-four-hour tip line and is asking anyone with information about Le's whereabouts to call 877-503-1950.

By now, fewer than seventy-two hours remained before Le and Widawsky were to be married. Although fearing the worst, the families still wanted to believe the best. With all their hearts, they prayed that somehow the wedding would go off as planned, that Annie Le would miraculously appear and she and Jonathan Widawsky would walk down the aisle, exchange rings, and be pronounced man and wife.

NINE

On Friday morning, with still no word from Le, University President Levin once again tried to quell rising panic on campus. He assured the Yale community that the FBI was coordinating the efforts of more than a hundred officers from four different agencies—the Yale Police Department, the New Haven Police Department, the Connecticut State Police, and the FBI—in an effort to locate Annie Le. He was certain they would get to the bottom of the situation soon.

Yale Police chief Perrotti sent an email to the Yale community reporting that the University was offering a $10,000 reward for information on the whereabouts of Annie Le. And investigators continued to interview colleagues, friends, and family.

But by Friday evening, the authorities reported that they still could not state definitively whether or not Le ever exited Amistad. They said they were continuing to review the surveillance video from surrounding buildings, but so far, could not come up with an image of her anywhere. They also revealed that they had looked at Le's computer and her e-mail for clues about what may have happened to her, but, they reported, nothing stood out as significant.

Two specially trained dogs from the state police were

brought back to 10 Amistad that evening—although authorities cautioned that after seventy-two hours, it would be extremely difficult for dogs to follow a scent. Then, widening their search, investigators donned Hazmat protective suits and pored through trash bins and a dumpster behind 10 Amistad Street.

But still, nothing.

Then, in a portentous turn of events, members of the Le and Widawsky families called the North Ritz Club in Syosset and told them that they were canceling the wedding.

Even for those who were most hopeful—those who were praying the hardest that Le would be found whole and unharmed—her disappearance had taken on a darker hue. It seemed that for now and for the foreseeable future, Le's wedding was not to be.

TEN

On Saturday, September 12, investigators from the Connecticut State Police Western District Major Crime Squad continued their search of every inch of the basement of 10 Amistad. They entered each room, walked down every corridor, checked the doors, the floors, the lockers, and the lavatories—but nothing noteworthy stood out until . . . an investigator scanning the ceiling tiles, in a desperate attempt to find anything that looked the least bit noteworthy, saw something that caught his eye.

One ceiling tile looked different. It was not as secure as the surrounding tiles—not flat against the others. It appeared that it had either been tampered with or needed to be repaired. The investigator pointed to it. His colleagues came quickly. With gloves on, one detective reached up and loosened the tile.

Inside the drop ceiling above the tile, the investigators saw something that took their breath away. Tucked in the space were a single low-cut white athletic sock, with hairs and what looked like bloodstains on it, and a rubber glove. This was the first indication that something ominous may have taken place in the basement of 10 Amistad. The investigators were momentarily speechless. *This was big. Two pieces of potential evi-*

dence. Quickly, the investigators collected the items, packaged and labeled them, and sent them out for DNA testing. *Could the stains on the sock be Le's blood?*

As the day progressed and investigators delved deeper into every crevice of the Amistad basement, more potential evidence was uncovered.

Detectives located a pair of Viking brand work boots "in the lower left cubby hole below a bank of lockers in a locker room" in the basement. The boots had blood spatter on them. One boot was missing a shoelace.

In the North Hallway outside the lab, the police came upon a blue short-sleeved hospital scrub shirt with bloodstains on the front left breast.

Then, while examining the rooms in the basement, investigators noticed "possible aspirated blood stains on an interior wall" of room G22. It appeared that someone had tried to clean off the spots. In the same room, investigators found a cleaning spray bottle with bloodlike stains on it, two small round reddish-colored beads, and hair fibers.

In room G13, where Le had been working with her lab mice, investigators noticed "a possible medium-velocity blood-like spray pattern on the wall." Again, it appeared that someone had tried to clean up the blood. (This type of blood pattern—medium velocity—is typically caused by a beating. *Velocity* describes the amount of energy transferred to a blood source [a body, for example] in order to create spatter—not how quickly blood flies through the air.)

The detectives immediately tested the stains on the walls of both rooms using presumptive chemical testing (an analysis of a sample to determine if it is definitely *not* a certain substance or *probably* is the substance; one such test turns a solution of phenolphthalein from clear to pink in the presence of blood). The result of their testing: The walls in both G13 and G22 showed a positive reaction for the presence of blood.

At this point, one would have to be in serious denial to think that nothing horrifying had taken place.

Then, in what many hoped was the lead that would point to the murderer, an article in the New York *Daily News* reported that on the previous day, the authorities questioned one of Le's professors in connection with Le's disappearance. It cited an anonymous police source, who stated that the professor had abruptly canceled his class on Tuesday, around the same time that Le went missing. There was a strong suggestion that a connection between the two might be found. An article in the *New York Post* titled "Missing Bride's Prof Eyed" contained a similar story, citing a report by Fox affiliate WTIC-TV in Hartford. A headline on the Fox News Web site said, "Yale Professor Questioned in Graduate Student's Disappearance."

For a short while—several hours, in fact—many felt comforted knowing that the police might have nabbed their man and that soon the authorities would be naming the killer.

However, as soon as the university got wind of the article, University Vice President and Secretary Lorimer vehemently denied that *any* Yale professor had anything to do with Le's disappearance. Lorimer stated that this "typical Fox News hysterical headline" misleads the public. The police were interviewing hundreds of people, she said, "and there is no reason to believe any professor is a suspect in Le's disappearance."

Lorimer confirmed that the FBI had received many tips, and she hoped that the university's reward of $10,000 would cause people to step forward with any information they may have. Lorimer added that Annie Le's vanishing was "the most perplexing mystery." She continued, "As I am sure you understand, at this delicate time it is particularly unhelpful to begin speculating or jumping to conclusions. If it does develop that a crime occurred, we want to do everything to ensure that the investigation proceeds as swiftly and completely as possible." And then, in an ominous conclusion, Lorimer said, "At a certain point in time, you start wondering what sort of positive storylines there could be here."

As the afternoon continued, a new rumor started to spread around campus. A report aired on Fox WTIC-TV declared that Le's body had been located. Supporting that rumor, two Yale police officers reported that 10 Amistad was now a crime scene.

The Yale community was buzzing with questions. *Was Le really dead? Where was she found? Who was the killer? Had he been apprehended?* It seemed as if the four-day agony of waiting for word on Annie Le's disappearance was about to come to a resolution—albeit, not the one anyone was hoping for.

A press conference was scheduled for 5:30 p.m. with agents from the FBI, the Yale Police Department, the New Haven Police Department, and the Connecticut State Police. Expectations ran high that the mystery had been solved, and that the healing could soon begin.

Yale Secretary Linda Lorimer was the first to speak. She stated that she was in contact with the Le family, who had arrived from California, and that the university had assured them that it was doing everything it could to help them. The family, she reported, asked the public to respect their privacy. "The investigation is at a very difficult stage. It's just not right for them [referring to officials who would be speaking next] to speculate."

Kimberly Mertz, special agent in charge of the FBI in Connecticut, took over the microphone and swiftly dashed any hopes about a quick resolution, stating, "We are not in a position today to conclude whether this is a missing persons case or whether criminality is involved. We have conducted numerous interviews, and I can assure you no lead is going uncovered."

The crowd was oddly deflated. It seemed that the news everyone had "hoped" to hear would not be forthcoming.

Mertz continued, speaking directly to the rumor that a body had been located. "I will categorically say a body has not been found." But, she continued, "Items that could potentially be evidence have been seized," although these items have not been "associated" with Le. Mertz would not confirm exactly what had been seized—except to say that bloody clothes and other items had been "retrieved from a ceiling in the basement of 10 Amistad"—nor would she reveal why the authorities felt the items could potentially be evidence.

James Perrotti, Yale Police Department chief, spoke next, saying that Yale was fortunate in that it had so many cameras outside Amistad. He emphasized the $10,000 reward and the FBI tip line: 877-503-1950.

In a question and answer session, an audience member asked, "What was Le doing and with whom was she interacting at 10 Amistad Street the morning of her disappearance?"

"I am not going to provide that timeline," Mertz replied.

When another person asked about the fire alarm that went off the morning of Tuesday, September 8, Mertz said that she had no comment, except to say that the surveillance cameras were still being scrutinized.

Lorimer emphasized that the authorities were continuing to search Amistad and that bloodhounds had been called in to search Dumpsters in the area.

And then, almost abruptly, the authorities said that

was all the news they had, and the press conference was over. Dozens of reporters and hundreds of students and staffers looked at each other not knowing whether what they had heard was "good" or "bad" news. If, in fact, the items in the ceiling were *not* linked to Le, then it was potentially good news. However, if the blood *was* linked to Le, it was definitely bad news. The fact that a body had not been found was good news: Le might still be alive. Yet, every moment that Le remained missing felt like a time bomb ticking toward an explosion.

That night, blood-sniffing dogs and their handlers were once again brought to the basement of Amistad. Meanwhile, FBI agents and state troopers in Hazmat suits were searching the waste processing plant in Hartford, using Bobcat tractors and dogs. Their task was daunting. Anywhere from 2,500 to 3,000 tons of municipal garbage was located there. Bill Reiner, FBI agent, said that the officials were "following the trash" that left 10 Amistad. They stayed throughout the night.

Speaking to the media by telephone, President Levin said, "As far as I know, we cannot make inferences about what happened to [Le]."

A police source questioned about the potential evidence found in Amistad said that the blood found on the items of clothing could be either human or animal and that officials had sent them out for testing and analysis to determine its origins. Authorities stated that no arrest was likely until DNA came back from analysis.

The wheels of the investigation were now turning around the clock, but to those who were anxiously anticipating news of Le's fate and whereabouts, it felt like being in limbo. The waiting, the not knowing, it was agony. No one could guess when there might be a resolution.

Saturday night—traditionally a big party night at

Yale—was eerily quiet. Students hung around outside Amistad, some bringing flowers, others leaving candles, and many hugging each other, waiting with diminishing hope that their fellow student would magically appear. It was not lost on anyone that tomorrow was to have been Le's wedding day.

ELEVEN

Although students and professors attempted to conduct business-as-usual, that was not really possible. Since Le's disappearance, a black cloud of anguish seemed to have enveloped the campus, changing lively discussions to dire pronouncements; transforming vibrant smiles to frozen frowns; and turning energetic steps into foot-dragging shuffles.

At 10:30 a.m. on Sunday, September 13, downtown New Haven's historic Battell Chapel was filling up with people wanting to find a safe place to express their fears and to pray. Battell was a student-oriented church where faculty, students, neighbors, and all visitors came to pray and reflect.

Reverend Ian Buckner Oliver spoke to the congregants. He said that the preceding week "has tested many people in many different ways. It has brought up a lot of fears for people. It has brought up a lot of worry and concern for [Le] and for all our safety." He offered a moment of silence: "For Annie, and her family, who have arrived here in New Haven; for her fiancé, on this, what would have been their wedding day. Let's lift them up in our prayers."

With the events of Saturday clearly on their minds, the professors and students gathered at the chapel that morning looked grave and despondent. The fact that their friend and classmate was to have been married that day made fate all the more cruel.

In contrast to the silence in the church, 10 Amistad was buzzing with activity.

Lead investigators—including special agent Kimberly Mertz in charge of the FBI in Connecticut and Yale Police chief James Perrotti along with Assistant Chief Ronnell Higgins—entered the basement of 10 Amistad through a loading dock.

Then a state police Major Crimes Squad van was driven down the ramp and into the basement.

K9s were brought into the building for another walk-through.

Directly across from 10 Amistad, alongside a green open area known as Amistad Park, three Connecticut State Police cars were parked. Troopers in the drivers' seats kept their eyes peeled on the comings and goings of everyone.

Another trooper was running alongside the fence of the park, a search dog in tow.

Investigators were standing guard over two trash containers from a Church Street South location, waiting for teams to search through them before releasing their contents to garbage trucks headed for the Hartford waste treatment plant.

An FBI truck, a Chevrolet Suburban, and several state police cruisers were parked outside the Connecticut Resources Recovery Authority building in Hartford, continuing to follow the trail of any trash that had been taken from 10 Amistad.

The police were honing in on Amistad with laser focus. It was the epicenter of an astonishing burst of investigative energy. What exactly was going on?

* * *

In the afternoon, New Haven police chief James Lewis held a news conference. He reported that after their thorough searches over the past few days, the authorities now had in their hands around 150 pieces of evidence. He revealed that they had also interviewed over 150 people, and had taken an even closer look at the surveillance video, using more sophisticated equipment. Although the authorities felt they were making progress, he said that they were still confronted with the fact that after five days of searching, Annie Le still was nowhere in sight.

However, all that was about to change.

At 4:30 p.m., Sunday, as investigators continued their search of 10 Amistad, several police officers entered a locker room on the lower level. Immediately, they smelled a foul odor. From their years of being on the force, they knew exactly what the smell was, and it was not rotting garbage. It was most definitely the smell of a decomposing body.

Cadaver K9s were immediately brought in. Max, a German shepherd trained in cadaver recognition, was the first to arrive, with State Trooper Nick Leary as his handler. On previous days, Max had searched through garbage from Amistad that had been sent out for incineration, but he had not signaled that he smelled anything suspicious. But Max's reaction now was totally different, alert and insistent. As soon as he arrived in the locker room, he dragged his handler to an area behind a toilet—where he barked, then sat at attention, and stared. There was nothing obvious in sight, but it was an ominous sign. Max was trained to react to only one thing—the smell of human remains.

The investigators saw that there was a panel—about the size of a computer screen—located directly above and behind the toilet. Immediately they removed it.

The area was a mechanical chase, used to house pipes and other equipment between floors. Once the door was off, they knew they were about to witness something monstrous.

At first, they saw bloodlike smears through the opening. Then they noticed blood behind the panel's frame, blood on the pipe insulation, and blood on the access panel itself. The chase itself was narrow, only about eight inches wide. But as they continued probing, they could see that insulation had been taken out from inside the opening. Looking deeper, they came upon what they had hoped they would never find—the lifeless body of a female.

Veteran detectives gagged as they began the painstakingly slow and gruesome process of removing the body. The corpse was that of a small woman, they noted, and she was wearing surgical gloves with her left thumb exposed.

As they carefully removed the body from the chase, the investigators found several items in the chase with her, including a green-ink pen, a stained lab coat, and an ankle-type sock.

As soon as the body was removed, the police covered it, and it was driven to the State of Connecticut Medical Examiner's Office.

Several hours after Le and Widawsky were to have said their wedding vows, the news that nobody wanted to hear was about to become public. In spite of the time that had passed, everyone was still hoping for a miracle. *Perhaps there had been a glitch in communication. Maybe signals had gotten crossed, and Annie Le would come strolling back into their lives, as if nothing out of the ordinary had taken place.* But that simply was not to be.

It was the responsibility of the police to deliver the

news. In a four-minute press conference at New Haven Police Department Headquarters, New Haven Police Department Assistant Chief Peter Reichard told the media, "We did locate the remains of a human. . . . We are assuming that it is [Le] at this time." He added that members of the Connecticut State Police Major Crimes Unit discovered the body inside a recess, called a chase, used for utility pipes and cables behind a wall of a basement laboratory. Reichard stated, "New Haven police would now be taking over the case [because it was a homicide and within the New Haven police district jurisdiction] from a missing persons one to a homicide investigation." He added that the FBI, Yale Police Department, and Connecticut State Police were going to remain to assist in the investigation. Reichard stated that the killing did not appear to have been a random act, but he offered no further information as to how he came to that conclusion, nor did he give any details as to the cause of death. Amistad was immediately declared the site of a homicide investigation, and the building was sealed.

When Le's high school friend Cierra Montes heard the news, she said it was like watching a horror movie— that Le should go missing during the week before her wedding and that her body was located on the night she should have been holding on to her partner for life in a wedding dance. It was beyond comprehension.

That evening, Le's brother Christoper wrote on his Facebook page: "The human race has failed. I love you, my one and only sister Annie."

That evening, on CNN's true-crime show *Nancy Grace*, Grace went "straight out" to CNN reporter Mary Snow, at Yale medical school. Snow reported that police were keeping tight-lipped but that all indications pointed to

Le's killing as being an inside job. However, she added, the medical examiner said he would not release the cause of death in order to facilitate the investigation. Snow reported that a vigil was being held for Le and that security had been tightened. She said that President Levin stated that there was an abundance of evidence and "he was confident that the killer would be apprehended." Snow then pointed out that Amistad was one of the newer buildings in the area, with state-of-the-art technology in terms of security cameras. Incredulous, Grace screamed, "BS!" Citing the fact that there were no cameras *inside* the building, Grace scoffed at the idea that the building was as secure as it might have been. If the security in Amistad was so state-of-the-art, Grace wondered, how did the killer get away with murder?

Le's brother, her uncle James Bui, her aunt Ngoc-Tuyet Bui, Jonathan Widawsky, and his family met privately with Yale president Levin. The president later said that the meeting was "one of the hardest things he has ever had to do."

At 9:15 p.m., President Levin sent an email to the Yale community. The subject line was "Tragic News":

It is my tragic duty to report that the body of a female was found in the basement of the Amistad Building late this afternoon. The identity of the woman has not yet been established. An identification and autopsy will be undertaken by the Connecticut Office of the Chief Medical Examiner. Our hearts go out to Annie Le's family, fiancé and friends, who must suffer the additional ordeal of waiting for the body to be identified. I have met again with her family and conveyed to them the deeply felt support of the Yale community. Law enforcement officials remain on the scene; this is an active investigation, and we hope it is resolved quickly. The University has again pledged its full resources and cooperation to assist all the authorities in their work. I will update you as soon as there is more information. Richard C. Levin President

Later that night, President Levin spoke briefly to students, professors, and reporters outside Woodbridge Hall. He said that the investigation would continue and that he believed the situation would be "successfully resolved." He told the crowd that he would not answer any questions. "Now is instead a time for compassion, for condolences, for coming together as a community." He stated solemnly, "This is as bad as it gets."

The six-day search was over. The ending could not have been more heartrending.

The news barely had time to settle in when the police and FBI began to come under attack for the way they handled the case. Authorities from all over the country began to weigh in. Some noted that for almost a full six days, from Tuesday, when Le was last seen at Amistad, until Sunday, when her body was discovered, the Amistad building remained open to students, faculty, and staff—all of whom were allowed to enter with their Yale IDs. The authorities said they were shocked that the area hadn't been sealed off immediately after Le was reported missing. Some said that intentionally or unintentionally, evidence could have been removed or unwittingly contaminated.

Two *Yale Daily News* reporters stated that while the FBI and other authorities were combing the labs, they showed their IDs to a security guard and gained entrance to the building. "That's not supposed to happen," said Henry Lee, a retired commissioner of the Connecticut Department of Public Safety and a director of the Henry Lee Institute of Forensic Science at the University of New Haven. "That's a no-no."

In defense of the New Haven Police Department, Chief James Lewis said that the authorities initially believed they were dealing with a missing persons case—not a homicide. They had no reason to believe that a crime had been committed in the lab. "We have missing persons all over the country all the time. You can't shut down a building for that." New Haven police spokesman Joe Avery said it was up to the Yale Police Department, not the New Haven Police Department, to shut down the building if they felt that that was warranted.

President Levin came to the Yale and New Haven Police Departments' defense, stating that law enforcement officials were "all over the place" in the first few days after Le went missing and that access to the basement had been limited before the entire building was sealed. He said that in general, researchers do not move their research laboratory animals, so students and faculty who were conducting ongoing experiments needed access to the labs. Levin also explained that it had been difficult for dogs to get the scent of Le because of the thickness of the wall behind which her body was concealed. "It was only after a number of days that the scent became detectable," Levin said. An architect who was consulted on the building of Amistad noted that the mechanical chase, where the Le body was found, had thicker walls than other parts of the building for fire code reasons. In addition, he said, it probably had steel framing, and because chases connect the different floors of the building, their walls would be thicker. No doubt, the material made it difficult for K9s or humans to find Le.

In addition to the criticism of the police, Yale itself came under attack, as people wondered why there weren't surveillance cameras in the basement or anywhere else within Amistad. Students remarked that once they entered the building, their cell phones no longer worked and soundproofed rooms made it impossible to hear a person calling for help.

It also didn't take long for the pundits to weigh in on who could have been the murderer. As soon as the body was discovered, everyone seemed to have already formed a strong opinion.

Criminal profiler Pat Brown, appearing on *The Early Show* and on *Larry King Live*, weighed in. Since Le never left Amistad, Brown said, "All the evidence is there." The bloody clothing would belong to the perpetrator, she declared, "and that's why it was stuffed up there in the ceiling tile, which would be fantastic because there would be evidence on that clothing, perhaps DNA from the person, so they'll at least be able to put this creep away." She added that the police will most likely focus on someone Le knew well, "a professor, another student, somebody who knew her schedule, knew where she was, and that she wouldn't have been afraid of when she was in the lab."

Brown went on to say that because Le had not gone to a dangerous location, but instead to a place where she felt safe, in her lab, "my guess is the only fault she could have is that she was too nice, that she was too sweet, and that somebody that she worked with, she didn't realize that they were obsessing over her. That's what my guess is in this. I don't see a serial killer. I see a guy who thought he was entitled to her and was angry that she was not choosing him and she was going to pick somebody else, and as her wedding day approached, he harbored that anger and took it out on her. And I bet she never saw it coming because she was just too nice a person." Brown ended her remarks by saying that Le's case "makes me cry. It's really depressing."

The Widawskys did not speak with media. They remained in seclusion.

An impromptu shrine of flowers and candles was set up across the street from the lab building at the entrance to the park.

Lucas Cheadle, twenty-six, a student studying for his Ph.D. in neuroscience interviewed right after he heard the news, said, "I'm freaked. My awareness of danger has definitely increased."

"It's pretty terrifying knowing that in a keycard-accessed building, in broad daylight, this could happen," said Casey Blue James '12. "It kind of makes me not want to go anywhere by myself."

"I'm not walking at night by myself any more. It could happen to anyone, anytime," said twenty-one-year-old student Natoya Peart.

Michael Vishnevetsky '10, a molecular biophysics and biochemistry student, said that things felt "different than how I usually feel" about going to the lab late at night.

"It's a frightening idea that there's a murderer walking around on campus," declared twenty-year-old Muneeb Sultan.

Some students felt differently. Kristin Dugan, who worked at Amistad, said she would conduct her life as usual. "Things happen; you can't stop evil," she said. "If evil's going to happen, it's going to happen anywhere." She said she never feared for her safety before Le was murdered, nor did she afterward.

Deborah Kiley of Deborah's Hair Loft in Huntington, New York, the person who was to have styled Le's hair—along with Le's mother's, Widawsky's mother's, and five attendants—was interviewed by the *New York Times*. She stated that she was praying for Le and her family. "I can't even accept it right now. I never forget a soul I meet. I was going to be part of a beautiful day, which is the most important day of a girl's life, other than the day she gives birth."

A neighbor of the Widawskys on Long Island showed a reporter a garland of flowers. "This is Annie's bouquet," she said sadly. "It's already wilting."

Late Sunday night, Dean of the Yale Medical School Robert Alpern told an interviewer that because access to the basement at 10 Amistad was so limited, "I think that it suggests it was someone who could get into that space. It certainly would be extremely difficult for someone from outside of Yale to get into that space. Not impossible, but extremely difficult." Thomas Kaplan, editor of the *Yale Daily News*, concurred. "That seems to point to someone in our community being involved in this."

And that thought—that it was someone "among" them—alarmed many Yalies even more. *Was the person someone they knew personally? Was it someone they may even be friends with?*

The thought was sickening. And it was also perplexing. Friends of Annie Le said they could think of no one who would want to hurt her. She was friendly with everyone, and she was open and honest. If someone had threatened or intimidated her, Le's friends and family would most definitely have heard about it. *Wouldn't they?*

TWELVE

On Monday morning, popular history professor John Lewis Gaddis projected an image of Annie Le on a screen in his class on the Cold War. He told the students that he had thought a great deal about what to do on this, the saddest day since 9/11. His first thought was to have a moment of silence. Then, he said, "But what I really want is not silence. I want you to call home and tell the folks at home that you're okay and that you love them."

Before the autopsy was performed, on Monday, September 14, the coroner gave the FBI the clothes that were on Le's body. As the authorities were looking through them, they saw a "round reddish-colored bead along with a broken string contained within the clothing of the victim." The FBI took photographs of all the items. Authorities were particularly interested in comparing the bead with beads they had recovered from various locations in the basement of Amistad.

Chief Medical Examiner Dr. H. Wayne Carver II performed the autopsy. Afterward, he made a public statement. He declared that the body found in the chase was, indeed, that of Annie Le. He stated that Le's death was a homicide. However, he said that he would not release the cause of death until the next day, Tuesday, at 3 p.m., at the request of investigators.

With the murderer still at large, the Yale community was understandably nervous. Lorimer tried to calm students, their parents, professors, and other staff by sending out an email. She wrote that the Amistad Building would be closed to everyone except for those "with essential responsibilities," who would be accompanied by law enforcement officials when they entered and while they remained inside. And when the building reopened, she wrote, added security would be in place both inside and outside the facility. She said grief counselors would be available, and that the Chaplain's Office would put students in touch with a person of their faith to speak to. She reported that the area around Amistad was being even more closely monitored now, with increased patrols and added security officers. She also stated that two streets near Amistad were closed off with yellow police tape, and that the Sterling Hall of Medicine was also being closely monitored.

Deputy Secretary Martha Highsmith, overseer of campus security, spoke to the media saying that authorities knew exactly who was in the basement at the time when Le entered. The situation, she felt, would come to a resolution shortly.

In the morning, New Haven Police Department spokesperson Joe Avery stated that the police believed Le was targeted. He declared that he did not think another student was involved in Le's death, but he would not go into any details. "We're not believing it's a random act. That's all I'm giving you right now."

At 1 p.m., Avery offered more information. He claimed that although there were "no suspects," authorities were concentrating their attention on "a few people of interest who were being very closely followed" and who were known to have been in the building at the time of Le's disappearance.

Several media outlets went a step further. They reported that police were interviewing a possible suspect, who had supposedly failed a polygraph and who had scratches on his body, which were described as defensive wounds. The *New Haven Register* and WNBC-TV both reported that the suspect was a lab technician. Crimesider, an Internet site geared to all things true-crime related, citing an anonymous police source, also reported that a person of interest—a lab technician—was being closely monitored.

It sounded like the authorities were closing in on a possible killer.

A meeting was convened for members of Yale's medical school community, who, like others on campus, were anxious to hear the latest news: *Was a person in custody, or was the killer still at large?* To accommodate the unexpectedly large number of people who came—over 550—the meeting was moved from the Hope Memorial Building to the Harkness Auditorium. No arrest had been made, said President Levin, but he assured the attendees that their safety was not at risk. He said that because of the security cameras at the entrance and exit of Amistad, the authorities had a "very small pool" of suspects they were following. "The appropriate people are being monitored, and there is no reason to worry about working in Yale research facilities. The people in the basement aren't going to cause any trouble until the matter is resolved." When students asked for additional surveillance cameras to be installed, Levin said sadly that cameras might not have been enough to save Le.

"No amount of hardware can overcome the darkness of the human soul when an evil person decides to do a terrible thing," said Levin.

* * *

Although the bells at Harkness Tower, Yale's most iconic landmark and one that contained the Yale Memorial Carillon, a musical instrument consisting of fifty-four bells, were undergoing a yearlong renovation, the Guild of Carillonneurs was given access to toll the bells to honor Annie Le. That evening, the stirring sound of the long-silenced bells tolled in her honor.

A candlelight vigil, lasting about twenty minutes, took place starting at 8 p.m. Over two thousand people gathered on the Cross Campus lawn. President Levin said, "I am reminded that we are an extraordinary community, a community of concern." He urged students to seek help for "this horrendous trauma."

Le's roommate Natalie Powers spoke about the loving and funny woman she shared her life with for the past two years. "She was as good a human being as you could ever hope to met. She was tougher than you'd think just by looking at her. It brings me a sense of comfort that God is in control and something will come of this. It's a comfort I think she would want us to have." Amid tears, Powers continued: "That this horrible tragedy would happen at all is incomprehensible. But that it happened to [Annie] I think is infinitely more so."

University chaplain Sharon Kugler, who had spent time with the Le family before the vigil began, invoked a prayer. Reverend Robert Beloin of St. Thomas More, the Catholic chapel at Yale, concluded the service with a benediction and a moment of silence.

Students began to hum. Soon, the hum turned into a song— "Amazing Grace." Tears flowed down the faces of many in the crowd. After the singing ended, a single violin played the same hymn, the sound emanating from Berkeley College, one of the twelve residential colleges at Yale.

Over one hundred mourners placed candles along the steps leading from Sterling Memorial Library to the lawn in a single file. Bouquets and candles were also lovingly laid around the fence leading to the building. As the candles burned, onlookers no doubt thought of a life burned out before its time.

Many students and faculty milled around for over an hour, offering hugs and words of comfort to one another. Although not all the people knew Le personally, her tragic ending touched them all. "I came to show solidarity to a fellow Yale student because we are a community. . . . The entirety of the school came together," said Yishai Kamin '12.

Anthony Diaz-Santana traveled from Ithaca, New York, to New Haven to honor the young woman he met while at the National Institutes of Health. He said he had kept in touch with Le via Facebook, and although they spent only nine weeks together, each considered the other a close friend. "This showing is a reflection of her impact on people . . . you see it here," he said. "She has brought a lot of people together."

And she did—but under such heartbreaking circumstances.

THIRTEEN

By Tuesday morning, exactly one week after Le went missing, no one had yet been brought into custody. Even with the hundreds of pieces of possible evidence, the 700 hours of video surveillance, and the hundreds of interviews, the police still had not made an arrest. It was disheartening to say the least, and many people were disturbed and frightened. *What were the authorities doing anyway?*

As the day progressed, the community anxiously awaited the results from the autopsy, which the chief medical examiner, Dr. H. Wayne Carver II, had stated would be revealed at 3 p.m. However, when Carver spoke to the media, he took an about-face and announced that he would not, in fact, be revealing the autopsy report. He said that he would not be making the contents public because the state attorney's office has asked for a delay "to facilitate the investigation." Carver stated that he could not say when the autopsy would be released and added that no further information would be forthcoming that day on the subject.

Police confirmed Carver's statements, adding that the prosecutors feared that releasing the autopsy could prejudice the case.

Many were frustrated that the whole investigation

seemed to be just slogging along. The community wanted to know what was being done to solve the murder, and they were becoming angry at the paucity of details that were being disseminated.

That evening, Dennis Smith, pastor of the Seventh Day Adventist Church in New Haven, was asked to speak for the Le and Widawsky families, although he did not know Annie Le or Jonathan Widawsky personally. Smith read a statement outside Woodbridge Hall on behalf of the two families. The families wished "to thank everyone in the community and around the nation for the thoughts and prayers," he said, and they would like to give special thanks to the New Haven Police Department and the FBI, as well as to other agencies for the "professional and compassionate manner in which they are conducting the investigation." The pastor went on to say that the families wanted everyone to know that "our loss would have been immensely more difficult without [everyone's] support." The pastor then thanked president Richard Levin and left the podium without answering any questions.

The rest of the evening passed quietly, somberly, with rumors swirling that an arrest was imminent. By ten o'clock, no word of an arrest or the name of a "person of interest" had been mentioned.

However, at approximately 10:25 p.m., all that was about to change. State troopers, along with FBI agents, were on their way to the Wharfside apartment complex in Middletown, Connecticut. When they arrived, two officers exited their car and knocked on Apartment 1A.

A gentleman answered the door. He was shown two warrants and then placed in handcuffs.

Who was this Middletown man now in handcuffs, and why had he been singled out?

PART
II

ONE

Raymond John Clark III was born on January 28, 1985, in Wallingford, Connecticut, located in the south central part of the state. He grew up in Branford, on the north shore of the Long Island Sound, eight miles east of New Haven, where his family lived in a working-class community. Painted gray, the family's rented house seemed to match the flagging spirit of the neighborhood. As the years passed and the nearby factory closed, the house deteriorated. In time, Clark's parents moved to a condominium in Cromwell, north of Middletown, where unemployment was below the state's average and income was above. According to a friend of the Clarks, who did not wish to give her name to a reporter, Raymond John Clark Jr. and Diane Clark were presently separated. Clark's mother worked in a Walmart across from her condominium. His father was retired.

Clark spent his freshman and senior years at Branford High, but attended Lyman Hall High School back in Wallingford for his sophomore and junior years. High school life agreed with Clark. He was not only good-looking, 5'9", and muscularly built, but he was also an honor student and an outstanding athlete—star pitcher on the baseball team and star quarterback on the football team. Known as competitive, talented, and versatile, he played hard and was all business on the field. Longtime athletic director at Branford High, Artie Roy, described Clark as a "quiet student who threw a mean knuckle-ball." Roy noted that Clark "was a seriously good pitcher and a good infielder. He wasn't a typical off-the-wall knucklehead kind of kid who bounced all over the place." Clark was competitive, Roy recalled, but he also respected authority.

One story passed down over the years about Clark was how during a baseball rite of passage, team members chewed tobacco. Of course, Clark joined in, not wanting to be the odd man out. However, after he put some tobacco in his mouth and started chewing, he got so sick that when he finally made it home, he raced into the bathroom, turned on the water, and took a shower with all his clothes on. Clark then proceeded to spend the night sleeping in the bathtub, fully clothed in his uniform. In spite of his precarious night, he managed to make it to school the next day—albeit quite late.

Clark had many friends, both on the field and off. Conor Reardon, a baseball player with Clark in high school, said that Clark was "a friendly guy, a person-able guy. I know that he had a tendency to be a little bit shy, perhaps, around people that he didn't know. And so, if someone had described him as withdrawn or aloof, they wouldn't necessarily have been way off the mark, but once you got to know him a little bit, he was personable, respectful, and friendly." Reardon went on to say that Clark "had a great sense of humor, over the top, bordering on manic. I really liked him." High school friend Cheryl Preneta remarked that Clark was good-looking and had plenty of friends. "There's nothing bad about him that I can think of at all."

Others at Branford High echoed the sentiments. Several teammates said they never recalled him having a short fuse, either on the field or off. Although his teammates knew he had a competitive streak and cared deeply about winning, they also felt he was one of the "nicest kids." Kelly Godfrey, who had known Clark since elementary school, remarked, "He was really quiet, but he was very friendly. He was easily one of the nicest guys in our class." High school friend Lisa Heselin called him a "jokester, kind of a class clown." Maurice Perry, who met Clark in first grade, called him "happy, athletic, and fun" and considered Clark his best friend in their early school years together. Perry said that Clark was calm, content, and seemed happy. He said that they spent a lot of time in later years in the weight room at high school. "Ray was one of the bigger kids on the football team. He was wide, well built, stocky." Perry said that Clark was quick to make a joke, and that he was cool. "If he was sitting here right now, you would have a good time."

While attending Branford High, Clark was involved with three different clubs. One was the Interact Club, in which he and the other members raised money to help the homeless. Another was the Cheers for Charity Club, which raised money for lymphoma and leukemia research. The third was the Asian Awareness Club, which, in an effort to help students understand multifaceted Asian cultures, the members prepared spring rolls and set up a trip to New York's Chinatown for Chinese New Year. (However, according to an article that appeared in 2009 on the *Hartford Advocate* website by Pang-Mei Natasha Chang, a contributor to the *New York Times Magazine* and *Saveur* and author of *Bound Feet and Western Dress*, Clark was never "really" in the Asian Awareness Club. Chang interviewed several of Clark's friends and one reported that the yearbook photos gave students a chance to "play around." He said that Clark and his buddies would vie for who could appear in the most yearbook pictures—and who could appear in the funniest one, "like the jock in the knitting club." Most likely, said Clark's friend, Ray got in the photo as a joke.)

Branford resident James Garrett, a retiree who lived two doors down from where Clark and his family lived, said, "There were no headaches [with Clark]. I never saw the police there or anything." He said Clark used to bring Garrett's beagle Tyler back home when he would break loose. "He was a good kid," said Garrett, "industrious and busy."

However, as well-liked and fun as Clark seemed to be, he also had a dark side.

Jessica Del Rocco and Clark dated in high school, when she was sixteen years old and he was a senior. In the beginning, they had a storybook relationship. "Everybody loved him," she said. "He was a good student. He was a great baseball player. He was perfect—he was charming, he was sweet, [he] took me out."

But slowly, according to Del Rocco, things began to fall apart as Clark started to try and control her every move. Clark would tell her what to wear, how she should speak, and to whom she should talk. He would tell her not to go to this place or that place and not to be friends with this person or that. He would even tell her that she talked too much, or that she wasn't talking loudly enough. He got so controlling that if things didn't go his way, "he'd make them go his way." She recalled that after one of his "episodes," he kept apologizing, saying he had good intentions, but then he flew off the handle again.

"When he would tell me I was breathing too loud, then I'd be in trouble," said Del Rocco. She admitted that many times, she was afraid of Clark. When he would get a certain look in his eye, she knew trouble was on the way. He would get very angry and "physical." Del Rocco said that she would sometimes do what he asked just to avoid a fight.

With arguments escalating, Del Rocco felt that the relationship wasn't worth the trouble, and decided that she wanted out. When she tried to break up with Clark, he confronted her in a "menacing way" and wrote "an unwanted message on her locker." Frightened, Del Rocco decided to get the school and the police involved. In 2003, she filed a police report. In it, she stated that Clark had forced her to have sex with him and that she was afraid of him.

When asked if she wished to press charges, Del Rocco decided against it, but said that she wanted the authorities to be aware of the situation. Clark was warned by the police that if he had any contact with Del Rocco, criminal charges would be filed against him.

For approximately two weeks after her visit to the police station, she said, she was escorted from school to her car. In time, things calmed down, and both she and Clark started dating other people.

After graduating with honors from high school, Clark decided he did not want to go off to college, but preferred to stay in town and find a job locally. He had his sights set on the Yale lab, where his sister, brother-in-law, and fiancée all worked. A position in the lab was considered plum, especially in the economically depressed neighborhoods surrounding Yale University. But procuring the job of technician was highly competitive. Vying for the position was a potpourri of people, from recently graduated high school students to laid-off workers to others with no advanced degrees or special skills.

In spite of the tough odds, Clark decided to apply. In

fact, he wanted the position so badly that on his application, he falsely reported that he had previously worked with animals on a farm, hoping that this information would give him the "prior experience" needed in order to submit an application.

Having a stellar resume was important, but procuring the recommendation of a relative or friend who already worked there was a necessity. And that was exactly what Clark did. In December 2004, Clark's sister Denise recommended Clark for a position in the washing center. Considered a tough job, the position required that a person scrape dirty cages, load cages onto a conveyor-belt washer, and lift forty-pound bags of food and bedding.

Clark was lucky. He got hired. He felt grateful and proud. From the first day he showed up at work, he performed flawlessly and tirelessly. His dedication, skill, and seriousness of purpose were noticed by his superiors, and eventually he was promoted to full-time animal technician.

Clark loved working at Yale, and he especially liked the camaraderie of being close to his fiancée, Jennifer Hromadka, twenty-three, a 2004 graduate of North Haven High School, his sister Denise, and her husband, Shawn Kent—all of whom had worked at Yale for years and had agreed to show him the ropes. It was a fun family affair.

In around March of 2009, Clark moved with Hromadka, a dog, and three cats to the Wharfside Apartments in Middletown, Connecticut, at 40 Ferry Street in Apartment 1A. Before that, they lived on the third floor of a rundown house on Ella Grasso Boulevard in East New Haven. According to Ann Marie Goodwin, their downstairs neighbor, Clark never said a word when they passed in the hallway they shared. Goodwin felt that Clark tried to control his girlfriend Hromadka and reported that Hromadka was very timid around him. Goodwin said Clark had "blank eyes." She said she never trusted or liked him. One day, after Clark reportedly chastised her son for leaving trash in the hallway, she said to him: "Yo bro, we deal with the smell of your fuckin' dog all day, don't be telling my kids about a bag of trash in the hallway."

By all accounts, however, in contrast to Goodwin's appraisal, while the couple lived in Middletown, Clark and Hromadka were quiet people who never threw loud parties or bothered any of their neighbors. Rick Tarallo, who lived next door to Clark, said that the couple was "really quiet" and that they lived with an older man, whom, he felt, could be one of their fathers. The couple would leave for work every morning, and return home every evening. One neighbor remarked on how much Clark loved his dog and said she would often see him taking it for long walks. She said that when she first met the dog, it was all excited and a little out-of-control, but Clark told her not to be afraid. "He's friendly. You could pet him," said Clark. And sure enough, the neighbor and the dog became good friends.

Even Hromadka's father liked Clark, describing him as "a quality man, a wonderful guy."

Good-looking, clean-cut, athletic, and fun-loving, Clark seemed like a perfect catch to Hromadka. They lived together happily and they worked together seamlessly. On their shared MySpace page, Hromadka and Clark posed in goofy pictures—in one, possibly for a costume party, Clark painted his face red, outlined his eyes in heavy black, and wore black lipstick with devil horns protruding from his forehead—and she gushed over her "wonderful boyfriend Ray."

Was Clark ready for marriage? A MySpace page he created in 2006, and then never used again, suggested he might not have made the most mature bridegroom. On his MySpace profile in the "About Me" section, he wrote, "Hello my name is homo ray I fart on people." And in the "Who I'd Like to Meet" section, he wrote, "your mom so I can [expletive] her." Under his interests, he wrote "porn" for movies, TV, books, and heroes.

The couple became engaged on New Year's Day, 2008, and seemed thrilled about the prospect of sharing their lives together. However, in a May 15, 2008, MySpace entry, Hromadka felt it necessary to defend her boyfriend against rumors that he was having an affair with someone else in the lab:

"My boyfriend, Ray, if you don't know him, has no interest in any of the other girls at YARC (Yale Animal Resources Center) as anything more than friends. He is a bit naïve, doesn't always use the best judgment, definitely is not the best judge of character, but he is a good guy. He has a big heart and tries to see the best in people ALL THE TIME! Even when everyone else is telling him that the person is a psycho or that the person can't be *trusted*. He thinks everyone deserves a second chance and has a hard time hurting people's feelings and it takes him getting burned to learn.

"This rumor of a 'fling' is probably the most stupid thing I have ever heard and really is not even worth going into detail about it. If you know what I am talking about u can probably (if you have half a brain) come to the conclusion that its [sic] all a load of BS."

What Clark might have thought of these rambling comments about him is anyone's guess.

According to the wedding website the Knot, they planned to marry on December 20, 2011. One entry read: "828 Days To Go."

* * *

At Yale, the position of Animal Technician 3, which Clark held in 2009, included the "ability to lift at least 50 pounds; to observe and evaluate animals for signs of illness; and to maintain, sanitize, and decontaminate animals' rooms." Another lesser-known part of the job was to search the area looking for neon green tags, which signified that an animal needed to be euthanized. It was then the tech's responsibility to take the animal to the basement, lock it in a cage, and turn on the carbon dioxide machine. Many considered that the most depressing part of the work. The pay for this level of duties was between $18.71 and $25.44 per hour.

Techs are "our eyes and ears in the animal room [because] without them, we really couldn't get done what we need to get done," said immunology Professor Mark Shlomchik. On a daily basis, techs not only cleaned animal cages and notified researchers if they saw any change in an animal's behavior or health, but they also provided the animals with food and water. Technicians were watchdogs, advocates for the animals, and guardians of the rules. They made sure that ethical standards were always maintained, even by the scientists in the labs. They checked, for example, that all researchers wore gowns and foot covers before entering a room.

However, the techs' jobs came with a downside. David Russell, who was an animal technician at Yale for eleven years, between 1997 and 2008, stated that stress came with the territory. "If there's something wrong, you are the one who is on the hook," he said. Techs "live in fear of being held responsible for someone else's sloppiness. A single lapse, like a dehydrated animal or unsanitary work space, could mean weeks of disciplinary hearing," not to mention weeks or even years of setbacks for the researchers.

For the most part, researchers and techs appreciated

each other's roles in the research process. In general, the two groups didn't socialize, but their relationships were cordial. They often spent hours together in the same confined space, so they mixed in obligatory ways, with a "please"; "thank you"; and "have a nice day." It was not unusual for a tech to email or call a researcher concerning his or her lab work, if, for instance, a researcher was not keeping his cages clean or not wearing coverings on her feet.

Although on the surface, it seemed that the two groups got along just fine, some students commented that there was often an undertone of dissatisfaction, or even disdain, between the two groups. Low-level, low-skilled, and low-paid workers attended to their jobs alongside high-level, highly skilled and sky's-the-limit potential folks. "They are in their world. We are in ours," said one researcher and fellow graduate student of Le's. "There are highly educated, awkward people working with a bunch of less-educated people with a [crummy] job, having to serve the needs of the first group. There was sometimes tension between the mouse techs and those who do the research. It's all about who is in charge."

In spite of any real or perceived tensions between the groups, both researchers and techs loved working at the lab at 10 Amistad Street. Located in the Hill neighborhood, it stood amid other concrete and brick medical school buildings, which had replaced a commercial and residential stretch of the neighborhood during urban renewal in the 1950s and '60s. Still standing from the "old days" in the midst of all the university structures was St. Anthony's Church and two old elementary schools.

Amistad was a brand-new building. Completed in 2007, it was a four-story, 120,000-square-foot, state-of-the-art "green" model for scientific research. It housed three interdisciplinary research programs: the Yale Stem

Cell Center; the Interdepartmental Program in Vascular Biology and Therapeutics; and the Human and Translational Immunology Program. An environmentally friendly and energy-efficient building, the facility boasted, among other features, a 7,500-gallon rainwater collection cistern, where storm water was collected from the roof, nonchemically treated, and then used to flush toilets and provide irrigation for the building; dual-flush toilets, which provided considerable water savings and were considered clog-free; recycled construction materials; occupancy sensors for lighting; energy-efficient light bulbs; and bike racks and showers, to promote biking to and from the building.

Amistad was home to around four thousand mice, along with many hamsters, cats, dogs, pigs, sheep, fish, monkeys, and gerbils. Every day, scores of researchers hunched over their cages, sometimes for hours, hoping to find the scientific advance they had been painstakingly seeking. And laboring right alongside them were animal technicians, doing jobs that freed up the scientists for their research.

People who worked with Clark in the Yale lab had differing opinions about him. One researcher, Lufeng Zhang, said, "He's a nice man always." Another researcher stated that Clark took his job seriously and wanted to follow the rules perfectly. Several people in the lab commented that he was extremely quiet, "preferring to look at the floor when he passed you rather than look at you."

Other co-workers had a more negative view. Some complained that Clark was an "unpleasant stickler for the rules who often clashed with researchers and considered the mice cages his personal fiefdom." One person labeled him a "control freak" and said Clark would get angry if lab workers did not wear shoe covers. "He would make a big deal of it instead of just requesting that they wear them," he claimed. A team leader reported that several researchers complained to him about Clark, stating that Clark had been rude to them: "He would berate them for minor infractions. Everyone enforces rules, but he enforced them in an officious manner." These complaints caused the team leader to alert Clark's supervisor.

However, considering his overall conduct and demeanor, nothing in the years Clark worked at Amistad caused his supervisor or the people he worked alongside of to be the least bit concerned about him as a person or about his job performance. *So what? He could be a stickler for rules. So what? He could be officious and demanding. He was just doing his job to the best of his ability.*

Was something wrong with that?

After all, his position was on the line if anything went amiss.

TWO

On Tuesday, September 8, 2009—the relatively warm, sunny day Annie Le went missing—Clark awoke early as usual, eager to begin his day at 10 Amistad. After putting on blue jeans, a dark-colored jacket with white stripes, and white shoes, Clark left his first-floor apartment at the modern four-story brick Wharfside Commons, a ninety-six-apartment complex that boasted "all of the extraordinary style and amenities you dream of . . . and more." With a state-of-the-art fitness facility, central air conditioning, cable-ready living, and "comfortable" clubroom, Wharfside was an ideal place to live, in spite of the fact that nearby were shabby-looking old houses due for rehab.

Clark slipped into his red Mustang for the half-hour drive to 10 Amistad. He enjoyed what he did, even if some people—perhaps jealous or snobby ones—referred to him as a "shit cleaner-upper," "mouse keeper," janitor, cage cleaner, or "grunt." He knew that as an animal technician at Yale University, he had a lot of responsibility and accountability.

After the twenty-mile drive, Clark arrived at 10 Amistad at 7 a.m. and swiped his Yale ID card to gain entrance to the building. He then signed in using his customary green-ink pen and writing his initials, "RC."

Sign-in schedule task sheets served as a record of where a tech was during the day and what he or she was doing. That day, Clark's assignment was to maintain the animals in basement rooms G13, G24, and G33.

During the day, Clark left the building several times— when the fire alarm sounded, for lunch, and for a break or two. Then, after completing his shift, he decided to wrap it up and go home to relax. He was exhausted.

Clark left Amistad to meet his fiancée for a quick cup of coffee before the half-hour ride home. He looked forward to spending a quiet evening with his fiancée, as usual.

The next morning, Wednesday, Clark went to work as always, arriving early again to begin his day. However, when he got there, the area around Amistad looked far different from how it had the previous day. Officers were fanned out across the medical school complex, checking IDs, interviewing students, and looking closely at all the buildings and surrounding areas. It had been approximately twenty-four hours since graduate student Annie Le had last been seen, and around twelve hours since her roommate had reported her missing. By now, the Yale police were all over the situation.

That morning, Officer Jennifer Garcia of the Yale Police Department was "responding to the basement at 10 Amistad" when a male voluntarily came up to her. He stated that he knew the missing person, Annie Le. Garcia was eager to hear what he had to say, because the officers had been advised to find out as much as they could from anyone who had seen Le the preceding day. Furthermore, Garcia knew that as each hour passed, the chances of finding Le alive diminished.

The man introduced himself as Ray Clark. He then volunteered details about what had occurred on the previous day. He stated that yesterday, he left Amistad at

12:45 p.m. Annie Le, he told the officer, exited the building fifteen minutes before he did—before the fire alarm went off. He said he saw Le carrying two bags of mouse food on her way out. That's all he knew about the missing Le, said Clark, and he hoped that that little bit of information might be of some help. Garcia hoped so, too.

Garcia wrote up the interview and passed it along to her superiors, as per instructions. Perhaps these details could point the authorities in the direction of the missing student.

After reading Garcia's report, which stated the time that Clark saw Le leave Amistad, the authorities located Clark and asked him if he would mind being interviewed. The detectives were desperate to find out anything they could. Clark immediately agreed.

The police began by asking Clark what he was doing at 10 Amistad on September 8. He told them that it was his job to maintain the animals in rooms G13, G24, and G33. They asked him about Le: Where did you see her? What time was it? What was she wearing? He said that he saw Le in G13 at around 10 a.m., wearing a brown skirt and a yellow lab coat.

When asked about his activities in G13, Clark stated he stayed in the room a short while on Tuesday, September 8, to do his clean-up chores and then went into other rooms to which he was assigned. He told the officers that he left the building to get some lunch at approximately noon and returned at approximately 12:30 p.m. He said that he witnessed Le collect some belongings and leave G13 between 12:30 p.m. and 12:45 p.m. "carrying her notebook and two bags of mouse food." He said that he left the building a little later, then returned shortly thereafter. Clark reported that a fire alarm went off sometime between 1 and 1:30 p.m.

The detectives were intrigued by the information

about the time Le left the building. They felt that this narrowed timeframe could help them locate Le on the video surveillance cameras. Thus far, they had not been able to find a photo of Le exiting Amistad.

By nightfall, after Le had still not been seen for over thirty hours, the entire Yale community was beginning to be deeply concerned, if not panicked. Adding to their alarm was the fact that the Yale Police Department had *officially* declared Le a "missing person" that day. Furthermore, in a sign that showed how seriously they were taking the situation, the Yale Police called in the New Haven Police, the Connecticut State Police, and the FBI to help with the investigation.

As of Wednesday night, four different police organizations, with over a hundred law enforcement officials, were on the case. It *was*, indeed, a serious situation.

On Thursday, September 10, Ray Clark went to work as usual. The campus was now dotted with flyers showing the missing Annie Le and asking anyone with any information to contact the Yale Police Department.

As authorities continued to question anyone who entered Amistad, they also conducted even more in-depth searches of the building, with K9s from the Connecticut State Police. Officers were now stationed at every entrance and exit of the building, as well as in front of and within many of the lab rooms and at various places along the hallways.

Sergeant Joy Jones and Officer Sabrina Wood of the Yale Police Department were assigned to G13, which measured approximately 16 feet by 10 feet. No sooner had the two officers arrived that morning and taken a quick look around than a young woman approached them and introduced herself. She said her name was Rachel Roth and she was a postdoctorate fellow and a co-worker of Le's. Roth said that something alarming had just caught her eye. Pointing to a box of Wipe-Alls on a steel pushcart in the corner, she asked, "Doesn't that look like blood?"

Officer Wood walked over to the cart to get a closer look. To her, it indeed looked suspiciously like blood spatter. Immediately, she called the FBI agents who were working in the building to come and take a look.

As Wood and Jones waited for the agents to arrive, a lab technician entered G13, then exited, then entered and exited several more times. During one of the times he was in the room, Wood and Jones observed him go to the cart and look at the box of wipes. They watched him as he then positioned himself between Wood and the wipes and turned to face Wood. He started to chat her up and as he did so, he leaned his body against the cart and moved the box of wipes from where it was, on the far left corner of the cart, to the far right corner. Now, the bloody part of the box was facing to the right-hand side of the cart, out of Wood's line of sight.

Presumably satisfied that he had deflected the bloody box from the officers' sight, the tech then began to scrub the floor under the sink near the drain, using an SOS pad and cleaning solution.

When FBI Agent Jim Wines and Special Agent Lisa MacNamara entered room G13, they asked the tech to wait outside so they could speak with the officers alone.

Wood reported to the agents what had just taken place, noting that the tech's action seemed to be a "deliberate attempt to block her view of the box in question." Then, with her fingernail, so as not to compromise any evidence that might be there, she pushed the box of Wipe-Alls back to its original position. Sergeant Jones corroborated Wood's account. Both Wood and Jones reported that the tech had begun to intensely scrub several areas of the floor, even though to them, the floor looked spotless.

The tech in question was Raymond Clark. And while the "mouse wrangler" may have thought he had tricked the officers, it appeared that the he had actually fallen into their mousetrap.

A few minutes later, members of the FBI New Haven Field Office Response Team came into the room and collected the box of wipes, placing it in a secure bag and labeling it.

By day's end, the box of wipes was sent to the State of Connecticut Forensic Laboratory for examination and DNA testing.

At this point in the investigation, Le's disappearance was still considered a missing persons case. As of Thursday, there was no evidence of foul play, and the blood on the box of wipes and on the lab coat could have been anybody's, even a lab animal's. But now that Clark had been reported as acting strangely, the authorities decided the tech was a "person of interest." Although the police had been scrutinizing the card swipes of every student and employee who entered 10 Amistad on the days before September 8, on September 8, and on the following days—on this Thursday evening, they decided to take an even closer look at Raymond Clark's actions.

Poring over the records, the authorities discovered that on September 8, the day Le disappeared, Clark repeatedly used his key card in rooms G13 and G22, which was approximately 8 feet by 8 feet, and that the key swipes were "in close proximity to each other." They noted that this activity was significantly higher than his key card activity on previous days. Between August 27 and September 7, Clark used his key card in room G22 three times total. On September 8, he used it eleven times. Between August 29 and September 7, Clark accessed G13 only once. On September 8, records showed he accessed G13 five times. Authorities also noted that on September 8, Clark's use of his key card was significantly higher between 10:40 a.m. and 3:45 p.m. than it had been during the same time frame on any other day—for a total of fifty-five key card entries.

Looking specifically at Clark's entries to room G13 on September 8, records showed that he entered the room at exactly 10:40:59 a.m. At some point, Clark left the room, because at 11:04:37 a.m., records showed he used his key card again to access room G13. After that, there were no key card entries for Clark for forty-six minutes.

Records of Clark's card also showed that he entered the building at 10 Amistad at least ten times on September 8, including after hours—which was both an uncharacteristically high number of times and an aberration in terms of entering after hours.

By day's end, the reports showed, Clark had used his card to enter six rooms: G7C, G13, G23, G25, G26, and G33, indicating that he moved in and out of rooms that he was not assigned to that day and which, presumably, he had no business being in.

In order to ascertain if Le's card swipes on September 8 would shed light on her proximity to Clark on that day, the officers scrutinized the record of Le's swipes.

The records showed that Le had swiped her card three times on September 8. When comparing the use of her key card on September 8 with the preceding weeks, the FBI could find no difference in the number of swipes or in the places Le visited.

The last entry recorded on Le's card on September 8 was at 10:11:50 to access room G13. Her key card was *never* used again.

Not long after Le's arrival at 10:11:50, Clark's key

card was used to access G13 at 10:40:59 and then again at 11:04:37. Among the most noteworthy findings was that Clark appeared to have remained in G13 for over three quarters of an hour before swiping his card again.

After forty-six minutes of no swipes on Clark's card, Clark then engaged in a lot of movement among basement rooms. He accessed one room after another room, specifically, he traveled between G22 and G13 several times, before going to the men's locker room, G30g, where Le's body was later found.

Another fact that interested the authorities was that Clark's key card was the only one used that day to access G22 after Le's arrival in the morning. The authorities believed that if something of evidentiary value was located in that room, the case could be blown wide open.

With Clark now high on their radar, the authorities decided to check the Amistad sign-in schedule task sheets again.

On September 8, the sign-in sheet showed that a person using the initials "RC"—known to all as Raymond Clark—entered six rooms: G07C, G13, G23, G25, G26, and G33—the exact same information as was revealed in the records of his key-card swipes. All of the entries for "RC" for the entire day, except for one, were made in green ink. The last green-ink entry was written at 13:30 hours, for room G7C. The entry after that, which was to room G26 at 15:48 hours, had the initials "RC" once again on the sign-in sheet. However, this time, the initials were written in *black* ink. *What had happened to Clark's signature green-ink pen?*

With their senses even more attuned to Clark, the authorities now took yet another look at the over seven hundred hours of surveillance video—this time paying special attention to Clark's statement that Le had exited the building at around 12:30 p.m. However, as carefully as they scrutinized the footage, they could not find any pictures of Le exiting the building at any time around then. But the investigators *did* come upon something that intrigued them.

On the morning of September 8, Clark arrived at Amistad wearing jeans, white shoes, and a dark jacket with white stripes. Later, the surveillance video showed him entering the building after a break wearing blue scrubs with a reddish drawstring. Then, when exiting the building after the fire drill, Clark was seen wearing blue scrubs with a blue drawstring. And at the end of the day, the surveillance video showed Clark leaving the building in jeans and a dark-colored T-shirt. *Why would a person change his clothing so many times in one day?* wondered the authorities.

Even though the police were concentrating on Clark, not a word of what they had discovered thus far concerning him was leaked to the media. They may have feared that if it turned out that Clark had nothing to do with the disappearance, they would be accused of having had tunnel vision and of setting back the investigation. Certainly, they didn't want to ruin the reputation of the wrong man—something the police department had previously done in the Suzanne Jovin murder case, which still remained unsolved and which still haunted the local authorities. Or maybe they just wanted to give Clark more time to hang himself. Whatever the reason, for the time being, the information about Clark remained within the notes of the authorities and the walls of the police stations.

At this point, the Yale community believed the case was no closer to being solved than it had been on the day Annie Le disappeared—and that made them angry and nervous. It had been nearly three days since she had last been seen, and her wedding was only two and a half days away. Things did not look good.

By Friday morning, the authorities—which now included the Yale Police Department, the FBI, the New Haven Police Department, and the Connecticut State Police—were eyeing Clark with increasing suspicion. After all, he had volunteered information about the time Le exited Amistad on September 8, but detectives could not corroborate this through surveillance videos; he had moved a box of wipes that had blood on it, seemingly in an attempt to hide the stains from the cops; he had cleaned floor areas of G13 that did not seem to need cleaning; and his key card swipes showed not only a different pattern of entry to and exit from Amistad compared to the preceding days, but also that he seemed to have been the last person in G13 when Le was working there. On top of this, cops noticed bruises under his eye and on his arms, chest, and ear. When they asked him about the scratches during an interview, Clark reported that they came from his cats. *Hmmm.*

By afternoon, the authorities were so convinced that Clark knew something he wasn't saying that they decided to step up the investigation a notch. Yale Police Chief James Lewis asked John Valleca, head of the New Haven Police Department's narcotics unit, to tail Clark. Lewis felt that the New Haven narcotics unit had a lot of experience in surveillance, and they needed to have the best on the case. Six detectives from the narcotics unit were immediately assigned to keep tabs on Clark.

A medical student who worked alongside Clark that evening, about five feet from him for approximately three minutes at Amistad, later said, "I didn't sense anything different in his behavior from what I'd observed previously."

Perhaps the cops were on the wrong track after all.

However, due to the many times he was questioned by members of the FBI and various police departments, Clark sensed that he had been specially singled out as a person of interest in Le's disappearance. As a result, he and his fiancée decided that they, and especially Clark, needed some expert advice as how to deal with the situation, so they called David Dworski, a Fairfield Connecticut attorney whom Clark and his family had known previously—although it was not clear whether they knew him because of past legal dealings or through social interactions. Dworski's website noted that the attorney practiced "law with an emphasis on real estate purchases & sales; DWI defense; personal injury law; and criminal defense law." It also stated that he "presented and won the first Criminal DNA case decided by the Connecticut Supreme Court."

After discussing the situation with Dworski, Clark and Hromadka decided to sleep on the advice Dworski gave them before making up their minds as to whether or not Clark needed to lawyer up.

That evening, in a MySpace entry, Hromadka, most likely responding to to rumors that Clark might have something to do with the Le murder, wrote: "Who are you to judge the life I live? I know I'm not perfect and I don't live to be, but before you start pointing fingers, make sure your hands are clean!!" Later on the page, she added, "I have realized in the last few weeks the kind of people I want and need in my life. I have no time for your drama or your BS take it somewhere else. It is not my problem that you have no life! I am completely done! Don't come to me when your 'friends' stab you in the back I don't want to know about it cause I don't care."

And now, some wondered, were her *hands clean?*

* * *

On Saturday, September 12, detectives were closely watching Clark, as well as several other people, although none of the "persons of interest"—or anyone in the general public—had any idea that detectives were following them. That day, neither Clark nor the others did anything the least bit suspicious while under surveillance. For the police, it was now a waiting game. Would Clark or anyone else go somewhere or say something that would lead them to Annie Le?

By afternoon, many in the Yale community began to feel that this case might never be solved and that Le might never be found. As far as they knew, after nearly four full days of searching and interrogating, examining and scrutinizing, the police still had no suspects nor any clues to Le's whereabouts. It was depressing, disheartening, and terrifying.

However, just as some began to lose all hope, the police came upon something strongly suggestive of violence in the Amistad basement—although their discovery had nothing to do with the tail they had on Clark. While searching the lab, detectives saw a suspicious-looking ceiling tile and decided to see why it wasn't flush against the others. The police immediately removed it and located a glove and a sock with blood and fibers on it.

Who had hidden them there? And whose blood was on them? The authorities felt that they were definitely onto something.

Adding to the growing pile of possible evidence, later that day, in two separate locations, the police came upon work boots with bloodlike stains in the lower left cubbyhole in a bank of lockers, and in the North Hallway recycling box, a blue short-sleeved hospital scrub shirt with blood spatter on it.

The police decided to let this information be released to the public. After all, potential evidence had been located and in time, DNA would point to or exclude any persons of interest. It would not be a case of pointing the finger at someone who might ultimately be the wrong man. The fact that they were closing in on a specific person of interest, however, was a piece of information they did not yet reveal.

DNA testing on the bloody clothing would take days. However, it was a beginning and the police, along with the public, began to feel that this break in the case was pointing the way to the missing Le.

If Clark had been paying attention to the media that day, he no doubt would have had a few moments of breathing easy: a professor might be the murderer. But as quickly as that rumor began, it was definitively quashed.

When it came to light that within the basement of Amistad, work boots, a blue short-sleeved hospital scrub, an ankle sock, and a rubber glove had been located, all with possible blood stains on them, Clark may have had a heart-stopping moment. In fact, it was on this day that Clark hired David Dworski to be his lawyer.

By nightfall, although the case was taking a new and possibly encouraging turn, few people still believed that Le and Widawsky would be married the next day or that they would live happily ever after, as they had dreamed they would.

THREE

On Sunday morning, September 13, students gathered in Yale's Battell Chapel to pray for the safe return of Annie Le and to hear Reverend Oliver offer a moment of silence "for Annie, and her family, who have arrived here in New Haven; for her fiancé, on this, what would have been their wedding day. Let's lift them up in our prayers." That same morning, Clark left home and drove his car to play softball with his team, the Wild Hogs. Possibly, just having a lawyer to advise him was enough to make Clark feel relaxed and able to go on with his usual routine.

Of course, since Clark spent the better part of the day on the baseball field, he had no idea that the scene at Amistad was frenzied, with agents, K9s, and police special units combing even more diligently through every square inch of the basement, the trashcans, and the park outside the building. The situation on campus was definitely heating up.

Rain had soaked the field on which the baseball game was to be played, so the Wild Hogs were sent to East Shore Park for what was to be a playoff game. While they waited about an hour for another game to end, Clark, his fiancée, and his mother spoke with other teammates and their families. Clark was extremely friendly, playing with the kids of his teammates before the game began, according to Luz Viera, the wife of the Wild Hogs' coach. Speaking about Hromadka, Viera said, "She'd sit there with her wedding magazines, flipping the pages and looking towards the future, and letting the other girls admire her nice, big ring." Hromadka came to all Ray's games. Around 5'5", she had a round face, high forehead, brown eyes, and long straight brown hair, which she sometimes wore down and sometimes back in a tight ponytail.

Commenting later on the game, teammate Manny Perez said, "[Clark] offered to warm up. Nothing was weird. It was the same old Ray." Although the Wild Hogs didn't win, Clark played shortstop the same way he usually did—expertly, intensely, and showing no unusual emotion. Opposing player Vinnie Mauro said that Clark appeared at ease and not at all anxious. Mauro also said that Clark didn't interact much with his teammates, and, as usual, wore a Mets jersey bearing the name of third baseman David Wright.

Although, as always, the onlookers in the stands consisted of friends and relatives of the players, this time, several spectators sat in the bleachers who had never watched the team before. As it turned out, they were detectives from the New Haven narcotics unit tailing Clark—but they didn't stand out in any way and no one paid them any special attention.

After the game, one of the detectives remarked about Clark, "He's actually pretty good."

Later, in the afternoon, Clark visited his sister and brother-in-law and their two children in Higganum, Connecticut. Then he drove around fifty miles northeast of New Haven to the Hebron Fair, hosted each year by the Lion's Club. Features at the agricultural fair included animals, terrific food, animal and truck pulls, a carnival midway, and great music for "the entire family" to enjoy. After the fair, he returned to his family's home in Cromwell.

All during the time Clark was playing softball, visiting relatives, driving to the fair, engaging in the entertainment there, and then driving home, he had no idea he was being tailed.

Toward the end of the day, Sunday afternoon blues seemed to have descended over the campus. Everyone who was following the situation—which included every single person at Yale as well as millions of people throughout the country and the world—was aware that Le and Widawsky had been scheduled to be married at 11 a.m. that day and that no wedding had taken place. And now, seven hours after the "I do's" were to have been spoken and five and a half days after Le was last seen, there was still no sign of her. The situation looked menacing—and grave.

Throughout the day, investigators continued to inspect the video surveillance images of the main entrance to 10 Amistad. On the day Le went missing, September 8, they saw Clark passing through the door wearing blue scrubs several times. *Wasn't a blue hospital scrub found in the North Hallway with blood on it?*

Then, at around five o'clock, "bad" turned to "worse." Investigators detected a foul odor in a locker room on the lower level of Amistad. The smell was distinctive—decomposition—and it led the authorities to what they had prayed they would never have to see.

Le's dead body was found stuffed into a wall behind a toilet. It was heart-wrenching.

After detectives painstakingly removed the body from the wall, they took it to the medical examiner's office, where an autopsy would be performed. Soon, the whole world knew that Annie Le was no longer missing.

Mourning would begin. But so would a new sort of waiting game. *Would evidence on or around the body point the authorities in the direction of a killer?* Inside the wall, along with Le's body, investigators had found a green-ink pen, a stained lab coat, and another ankle-type sock.

By nightfall, police had cordoned off a one-block perimeter around 10 Amistad, and a homicide investigation, not a missing person's investigation, was under-way.

When Suzanne Jovin's parents learned of the discovery of Annie Le's body, they wrote a letter to Connecticut Governor Jodi Rell. "Tragedy has again struck Yale," it read. The Jovins pleaded for increased funding for the state's forensic science lab. "We hope that the person guilty of this terrible crime can be apprehended quickly, which was unfortunately not to be true in the case of our daughter," To this day, the murder of student Suzanne Jovin remains unsolved. The Jovins, Thomas and Donna J., said that they shared the agony of Le's loved ones.

Some people immediately began demanding the toughest of sentences for the murderer. "But what kind of punishment would fit killing someone and stuffing her in a two-foot hole in a wall?" asked Mayfield Kim in a post on a Facebook site dedicated to remembering Le.

When Bernadetter Durkin heard the news about Le, she wrote a letter to the *Yale Daily News*. In it, she told of the terror that hearing about Le brought back to her. She stated that her daughter had been a grad student at Yale when she was mugged at "knife-point by a masked man outside her apartment building at 8 p.m. on a November evening in 2004." She said her daughter was only fifteen feet from her "double security-locked building"; that she was always aware of her surroundings;

and that she did not take risks. Durkin stated that her daughter's purse, cell phone, and money were taken. She wrote how she immediately contacted the New Haven Police who, according to her, "did nothing." She stated that she called her daughter's cell phone, found out who the man was, and gave his name to the police. "Still they did nothing."

Durkin ended her letter by saying she was "so sorry for the loss that Annie Le's family has suffered and will suffer forever." Her final words were, "Something should be done about the lack of security or the lack of police follow-up when things happen."

One student, who asked not to be identified, said that when she heard the body was discovered, she decided to carry Mace in her backpack. "I just put it in my bag last night." Another said, "I'm not walking by myself anymore. . . . It could happen to anyone, anytime, anywhere." A third said, "We're all scared shitless."

Was that the way students at exalted Yale University were supposed *to feel?*

And what about Clark? Surely, he must have heard the news, which appeared on all major TV stations, that a body was discovered, and that it was that of Annie Le. How did *he* feel?

Had Clark turned on the TV that evening and tuned into Nancy Grace, he would have heard her guest, CNN reporter Nancy Snow, say that it was an "inside job."

How did Clark feel about that*?*

On Monday, September 14, John Valleca, head of New Haven's narcotics unit and the person leading the team of detectives tailing Clark, ordered the detectives to change their tactics from covert surveillance to overt surveillance. They walked in front of Clark's house with their badges clearly showing, trying to engage Clark in a conversation. But Clark never talked to them. From that point on, detectives reported, Clark abruptly stopped all his usual activities and drove from his apartment in Middletown directly to his parents' home in Cromwell. No doubt, by this time, Clark certainly knew he was a prime suspect in the disappearance of Annie Le.

Neighbors of Clark's stated that they saw Hromadka moving items out of their Middletown apartment that evening.

Clearly, movement was afoot.

In the early evening, Jesse Stanley, an electrician who had worked at Amistad since the building opened in 2007 and in various other Yale buildings for over twenty years, commented on how easy it was to open one of the electrical panels leading to the chase, the hollow in the wall where Le was found. He explained the chase was a "void in the wall used to take utilities from the top floor to the basement" and allowing access to wires and cables. With a screwdriver, Stanley said, or even "a butter knife," the chase could be opened. He felt that the body could have been stashed by "anybody who worked in that building"—a Yale employee or a student. "It's definitely someone that works in the building. The building's security system includes magnetic-card access." Stanley stated that some lab employees told him they had received visits from the FBI already, although at that time, he stated, he had not.

By the end of the day, with the media having reported that a possible suspect was being closely monitored—a person who supposedly failed a polygraph, had defensive wounds on his body, *and* was a lab technician—Clark must have felt the hot breath of the police on his neck.

FOUR

On Tuesday, September 15, for the second day in a row, neither Clark, his fiancée, his sister, nor his brother-in-law showed up for work at the Amistad lab.

That afternoon, a private memorial Mass was celebrated at St. Thomas More Chapel at Yale. Attending were Le's family; the Widawsky family; Yale president Levin and his wife, Jane; Yale vice president and secretary Linda Lorimer; high-ranking members of the Yale Police Department, the New Haven Police Department, and the FBI; as well as friends, colleagues, and mentors of Le. It was a solemn ceremony, with tears flowing down the face of nearly everyone in attendance.

It had now been a solid week since Le had gone missing—and all during that time, the authorities had not revealed to the public whether they had their sights on one person, several people, or no one at all. The police were doing everything they could not to let out any information that might compromise their investigation.

However, all that secrecy was about to change.

People living in Wharfside Commons in Middletown were aware that something unusual was afoot right outside their front doors. For the past twenty-four hours, surveillance cars were stationed all around the complex. Rumors were flying that someone within the complex might be associated with the Le murder. In fact, word spread that a killer might be arrested soon. Anxiety and fear ran high. *Who among them could it be? Whose next-door neighbor might be a suspect?*

That night, it became clear exactly why the police had been stationed outside the complex. At 10:25 p.m., detectives knocked on Apartment 1A. Raymond Clark answered the door and was immediately served with two warrants. Clark was then handcuffed and escorted to an unmarked silver police car. Neighbors leaning over the apartment building's iron railings cheered as a dour-looking Clark, wearing a white T-shirt and dark pants, was driven away.

At the police station, authorities began interviewing Clark the minute he arrived. For the next approximately four hours, Clark was interrogated. He allowed them to take DNA samples from his hair, his nails, and his cheek—requirements of one of the warrants. Immediately, the samples were sent out for testing on a rush basis. Clark also gave the authorities permission to search his apartment—a requirement of the other warrant.

According to the authorities, Clark was co-operative and talkative until . . . the detectives asked him about the scratches on his body. He replied that they were caused by a cat and by playing softball. When officials started photographing his injuries, Clark quickly asked for his attorney, David Dworski.

At around 3 a.m. Wednesday morning, after complying with both warrants, Clark was released into the custody of his attorney. Clark drove directly to a Super 8 hotel in Cromwell, around twenty-five miles from the Yale campus. His father was already registered in a room there and Clark quickly joined him. It turned out that Clark's father stayed there frequently; the staff and managers knew him well.

As soon as it became clear that the case would entail a lot of scientific evidence and a trial might be forthcoming, Dworski suggested that the public defenders' office would serve Clark better. During the week-plus that Dworski was involved in the case, he counseled Clark on possible scenarios and on how Clark might deal with them. Dworski met with Clark, his fiancée, his parents, his sister, and her husband five or six times for a total of approximately fifteen to twenty hours. Dworski ceased to represent Clark after Clark's first arraignment and bond was set.

Dworski later commented that when he first heard that Clark was in the crosshairs of the police—days before Clark contacted him—he was hoping that Le would turn out to be just another runaway bride. Then, after spending many hours with Clark and his family, Dworski commented that the Clarks were a loving family and appeared to deeply care about one another. He felt that Clark and Hromadka were very much in love with each other. To Dworski, Clark appeared to be an all-American young man, very nice, and extremely thoughtful. He emphasized the fact that Clark was "always eager to please." Dworski said Clark that would ask intelligent questions and listen to responses. "He couldn't have been more polite, appreciative, and respectful."

Above all, Dworski felt this was a tragically sad situation for everyone.

Clark was "always eager to please." Could those words hold a key to Clark's possible involvement in the Le murder? If it turned out that Clark was, in fact, the murderer, who might he wanted to have pleased? One could only wonder.

At the same time that Clark was being interviewed, New Haven Police Chief James Lewis was holding a news conference. Lewis reported that the authorities had taken in a "person of interest" to be interrogated. He said the person's name was Raymond Clark III. Lewis went on to say that if Clark cooperated and gave the police what they asked for, he would not be detained. Lewis stated that Clark was handcuffed because detectives had to gather DNA evidence from his hair, fingernails, and saliva and they "did not want anything tampering [with] the process." Lewis stated that authorities were still looking at several other people who accessed the lab on the day Le disappeared. "We are making sure there are not any other suspects, making sure we don't have tunnel vision." He said that other people who had used the lab and the building had already voluntarily submitted DNA samples for police. Lewis added that by the end of the week, Clark would either be exonerated or arrested, after his DNA was compared to the over 250 pieces of evidence collected from the crime scene. There will be no arrest, said Lewis, until "one match of a person at that location" takes place.

At around 5:30 a.m., two more search warrants were signed. They permitted authorities to search Clark's red Ford Mustang and to further search his apartment at 40 Ferry Street in Middletown for items not included in the search warrant executed Tuesday night. No warrant was issued for Clark's arrest, so his status as a "person of interest" had not officially changed to "suspect."

Around 6 a.m., Wednesday morning, more than twenty law enforcement evidence-gathering officials stormed Clark's apartment to conduct a thorough search. Police were hoping that some of the evidence they had already picked up from the lab would match evidence they were gathering from Clark's home. The New Haven Police Department, now in charge of the homicide investigation, set up a card table outside Clark's apartment door to sort through items.

By around 6:45 a.m., with the sun just beginning to rise, police were taking down the yellow police tape that surrounded the Wharfside apartment complex. Clark had not returned home.

At 9 a.m., the media was in a frenzy of anger and passion. The authorities refused to reveal what was contained in the warrants that Clark had been served with. New Haven State's Attorney Michael Dearington stated adamantly that he would not disclose that information, nor would he reveal the name of the judge who signed them. He said that the warrants were sealed because releasing them might "compromise the investigation."

According to Dearington, sealing warrants was a common and acceptable practice. "This goes on all over the country all the time. There's nothing unusual about it. It's as commonly accepted as the validity of the U.S. Constitution."

Harvard Law professor Alan Dershowitz, Yale Law '62, vehemently disagreed. "They cannot keep secret the name of the judge," he told the media. "There's no conceivable reason for that. That sounds like Iran. That's not America." Dershowitz was also surprised that Clark had been handcuffed on Tuesday night when he was taken to the police station on just a search warrant. That is a "completely and totally unconstitutional search and seizure. If there are handcuffs, then it has to be an arrest, which has to be based on probable cause and can't be based on being a person of interest."

Yale Law professor Steven Duke LAW '61, who specialized in criminal procedure, disagreed. "If the search warrant authorized the police to take Clark into custody, standard procedure required them to handcuff him. Legally, however, once he is handcuffed, he is under arrest, even if the police still label him 'a person of interest,'" said Duke. "The distinction between being in custody and being under arrest is thinner than an onion skin."

According to David Zlotnick, a former federal prosecutor who was teaching law at Roger Williams University in Bristol, Rhode Island, keeping information secret helps the investigators know, first of all, what buttons to push on the person being interrogated, and it makes sure they haven't tainted the investigation. "Secrecy," he said, "is useful." The less authorities tell suspects about what they know, the harder it is for suspects to make up a fake cover story or alibi.

In the afternoon, around ten hours after Clark had been released and two and a half days after Le's body had been discovered, a spokeswoman for the medical examiner's officer released Le's cause of death—finally. She stated that Le died from "traumatic asphyxia" caused by "neck compression."

Experts consulted on exactly what that meant stated that it could indicate "a choke hold or some other form of suffocation caused by a hand or an object, such as a pipe."

At last the public now knew how Le had died. One huge question had been answered. But at least two haunting questions remained: Who was the murderer, and why did he, or she, do it?

At a 5:30 p.m. news conference, Lewis offered an update. He said that the police were finishing up processing the building at 10 Amistad, including processing the water drains. If someone had tried to flush evidence down a toilet or a drainpipe in the floor, or rinse it down a sink, the evidence could still be found in the drains and pipes. He said that the authorities were prioritizing the hundreds of items they had previously seized. DNA tests were being expedited "as we speak. I could get the results in thirty minutes or it could be hours." He said that the DNA "could lead us to someplace immediately. We are still interviewing some people, but the basis of the investigation is focused on one person, but we don't want to be accused of tunnel vision. Until everyone is completely eliminated, we are keeping track of everyone."

Lewis went on to say that four search warrants had been issued thus far, and more were likely to come. He added that the police had been "monitoring" Clark for the past several days and always knew where he was. Lewis admitted that the police were monitoring other people as well, but the only search warrants issued thus far in the case were those involving Clark. At this time, added Lewis, "We have no authority to detain him in any way." Lewis said that Clark answered the police's questions at first, but later stopped and asked to retain a lawyer. "It's all up to the lab now. The basis of the investigation now is really on the physical evidence."

Reporters staked out at the Higganum, Connecticut, house where Clark's sister and brother-in-law lived stated that the blinds were drawn and two people in hooded sweatshirts raced out of the house and into the back seat of a black SUV at approximately 6 p.m. Two adults were reportedly already in the front seat. Clark's sister and brother-in-law were carrying suitcases, said one neighbor. "I thought they were going on vacation. I saw them leaving . . . with travel bags like they were in a hurry."

President Levin spoke to calm the nerves of the Yale students, staff, and faculty, who were only too well aware that a killer, who strangled a promising graduate student right on the campus and within her own lab, was still on the loose. "This really is in the hands of law

Annie Marie Le lived on the third floor of this house in the East Rock neighborhood of New Haven with her roommate Natalie Powers and several other housemates. It was from here that she would take the Yale bus to college each day.

Photo by Stella Sands

On September 11, 2009, a billboard on Interstate 91 in New Haven, Connecticut, featured a photo of missing Yale graduate student Le. She was last seen alive on September 8 in her laboratory at the Yale Medical School complex.

AP Photo/Thomas Cain

On September 12, 2009, a sign posted by two Yale graduate students hung in front of 10 Amistad Street, the building where Le's lab was located. Police patrol the entrance to Amistad.
AP Photo/Thomas Cain

These photos appeared on flyers that were distributed all over the Yale campus. The flyers asked anyone with information about Le to call the police. The photo on the right is an image from a surveillance camera located outside the entrance to 10 Amistad, taken on the morning of September 8, 2009.
New Haven Police Department

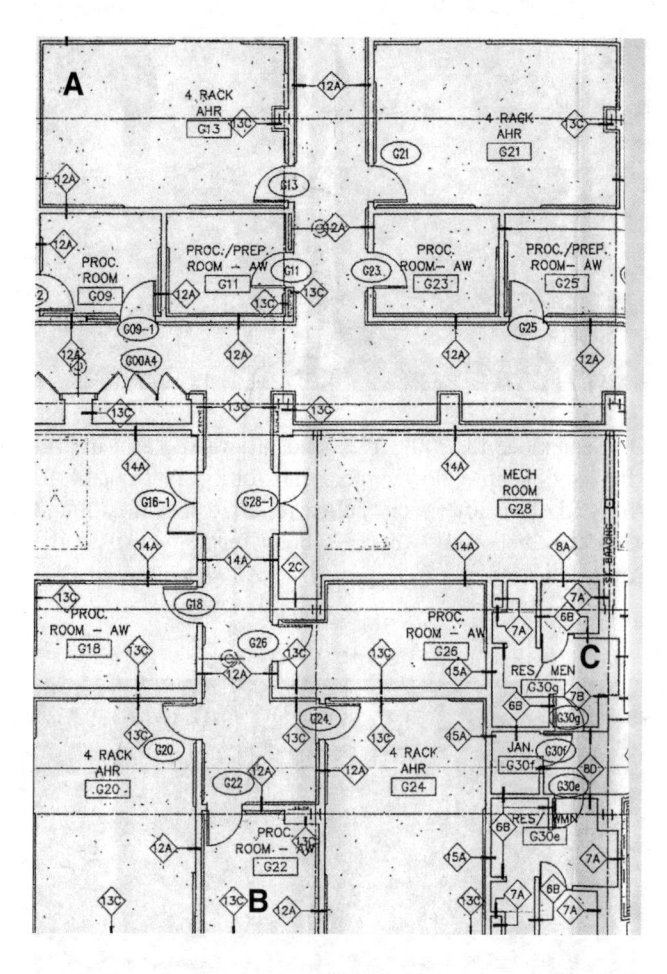

These blueprints of the Amistad basement show: A) the lab where Le worked, and where traces of blood were found; B) the lab room where aspirated blood was found on the wall; and C) the men's locker room where Le's body was hidden in the wall behind the toilet.

From the Building Department/City of New Haven, CT

On September 13, 2009, Yale students walked arm in arm after setting up a flower memorial for Le in front of 10 Amistad. That afternoon, police reported that they found what they believed to be Le's body inside a wall in the Amistad basement.   *AP Photo/Thomas Cain*

On September 14, 2009, Yale President Richard Levin spoke at the candlelight vigil dedicated to Le at Cross Campus at Yale.   *New York* Daily News/*Anthon DelMundo*

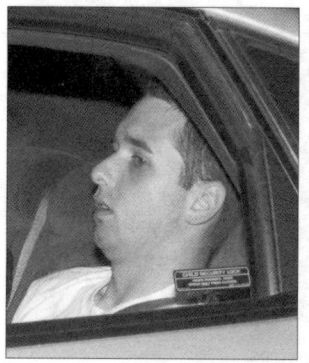

At approximately 10 p.m. on September 15, 2009, authorities executed two warrants on Clark at his Wharfside Commons apartment in Middletown, Connecticut.
New York Daily News/*Joe Marino*

Clark, his fiancée Jennifer Hromadka, and their dog and cats lived in the Wharfside Commons apartment complex in Middletown. They had moved there from East New Haven, approximately six months before the murder.

Photo by Stella Sands

On September 17, 2009, a police convoy left the Super 8 Motel in Cromwell, Connecticut, where Clark was staying with his father. Clark was handcuffed in the black car second from the right.   Yale Daily News/*Daniel Carvalho*

A media frenzy took place as newspeople descended on the New Haven Police Department at One Union Avenue to find out the latest on Clark's fate. *New Haven Police Department*

Clark being led out of New Haven Superior Court after being arraigned on September 17, 2009.

Yale Daily News/*Paul Needham*

This is Clark's mugshot, taken when he was arrested on September 17, 2009.

New Haven Police Department

On September 23, 2009, Le's fiancé, Jonathan Widawsky, wore a wedding ring as he left his home in Huntington, New York, for a ceremony honoring Le, to be held at nearby Temple Beth El.

New York Daily News/*Stephen Barcelo*

Family members, including Le's grandmother, attended Le's funeral mass at the Holy Trinity Catholic Church on September 26, 2009, in El Dorado Hills, California.

AP Photo/Russel A. Daniels

Pallbearers accompanied Le's casket after the funeral mass.

AP Photo/Russel A. Daniels

enforcement at this point, and so all we can do is be patient and wait for the results of the DNA test," which would be completed, he said, in twenty-four to seventy-two hours.

Although not everyone waited patiently, there was at least the hope that the DNA results would point directly to the killer.

FIVE

On Wednesday night, September 16, Larry King, on *Larry King Live,* began his show by saying, "There are major developments in the murder that has rocked the Yale campus." He then interviewed several people.

Standing on the Yale campus, Susan Raff appeared first. A reporter from WFSB-TV in New Haven, she stated that Raymond Clark was the only person of interest at the moment, even though the authorities had interviewed over 150 people. When King asked her why the authorities released Clark, Raff said, "At this point, he is not considered a suspect. He has not been charged with anything." She said that Clark was taken to the crime lab in Meriden, Connecticut, where the authorities "took all kinds of samples." Raff added that Clark was staying in Cromwell, the neighboring town to Middletown, and he was being closely watched.

King then called on Rocky Tuan, who had been Le's mentor at the National Institutes of Health, where Le worked for two summers. Tuan was currently living in Pittsburgh. He said that Le had received a very competitive scholarship from the NIH, and she had accepted it and went there for two summers to perform research. Tuan stated that Le was interested in tissue regeneration and development, so she chose to work in his laboratory, which was dedicated to that kind of research. Tuan reported that Le worked on adult stem cells. He said that Le was a "tremendous student, passionate, intelligent—a delight to have in the lab." According to Tuan, Le got along with everyone. She had a bright personality, was upbeat, and had a can-do attitude. If something didn't work out in the lab, he said, "she would figure out ways to get around it, get over it, ask for help." Le's goal, Tuan said, was to come up with methods to take care of diseases, particularly those that required new tissues to be formed. Le told him many times that she wanted to use biological knowledge to improve health and to help others come up with methods to treat diseases. Tuan recalled how excited Le was about the potential of the biomedical field. She wanted to be a professor in academia and even talked about coming back to NIH to be an investigator.

Thomas Kaplan, who King introduced as editor-in-chief of the *Yale Daily News,* was interviewed next. Kaplan said, "This is really a campus in shock. No one here was prepared for something like this." Yale had not witnessed anything like this since eleven years previously, when another student, Suzanne Jovin, was murdered. Kaplan said that even though so much media attention was being paid to the case, only the *Yale Daily News* was in a unique position to report on the story because its reporters had access to places other media outlets didn't: Yale students could enter campus buildings that outsiders could not.

Next, King called on Dr. Henry Lee, Chief Emeritus of the Connecticut State Police and founder and professor of the Forensic Science Program at the University of New Haven. King read to Lee that the official cause of death was "traumatic asphyxiation due to neck trauma." Then he asked Lee if that meant Le was strangled.

"Basically external force compressed the neck," said Lee. "It could be a strangulation. It could be manual. It could be a ligature [tying or binding]. It could be some heavy force that compressed the neck." Lee said that if marks were left on the neck, those could help locate the killer. But, he added, no specific information regarding that possibility had been released.

Lee said that it was definitely a DNA case. He added that the videotape, the key card, Le's activities, witnesses, and all the physical evidence would also help solve the crime. DNA, he stated, was a good tool to find the perpetrator, since it was more foolproof than fingerprints. In this case, Lee said, there were bloody clothes, and one needed to find Le's DNA on the clothing and Le's DNA under the perpetrator's fingernails or his DNA under hers. When King asked Lee about the terrible way in which Le died, Lee stated that her strangulation was "traumatic and tragic."

King next called on Pat Brown, criminal profiler and founder and CEO of the Sexual Homicide Exchange (SHE). He asked her if it was too early to profile a suspect. Brown said that there was a lot of good information out there to help figure out who did it. She said it was definitely not a random killing. "He knew this girl. He targeted her." However, she added, "I don't think it was premeditated." Brown believed that there was a great deal of rage in this crime. "Possible rape." Obviously, she said, the perpetrator had an interest in her. He liked her. He may have been obsessed with her, and she wouldn't give him the time of day. That made him terribly angry. If it was a serial killer, she said, he wouldn't have taken time to hide clothing and the body. He would have just run out. Perhaps, said Brown, the person was thinking, "Now that she's getting married and she's not interested in me, I'll show her. I think that was what was going on when this was happening." Brown felt they would find a lot of evidence under Le's fingernails because she no doubt struggled hard and fought against him—and the person they picked up had scratches on him. "This is going to be a heavy DNA case, in spite of all the circumstantial evidence," Brown stated.

King also interviewed Pastor Dennis Smith, spokesman for the Le family and pastor of the New Haven Seventh Day Adventist Church. (Smith had been asked by an Adventist friend of the Le family in California if he would be willing to be the spokesperson for the family. He agreed.) Smith stated that he wanted the community to know what a supportive and "loving family they are and very thankful for what's been done in their behalf." He added that he also wanted to do as much as he could to protect the privacy of the family.

King called next on Judge Joe Brown, host of TV's *Judge Joe Brown*. King asked, "Who do you think did it?" Brown's opinion was that it could have been an animal rights activist who had targeted the Amistad labs and was angered by all the "fuzzy little animals being experimented upon in the cause of medicine." He noted that animal rights activists had increasingly been engaging in "acts that Homeland Security calls domestic terrorism." Perhaps, Joe Brown suggested, Le had walked in on something unexpectedly—and paid the price.

When Pat Brown heard Joe Brown's comment, she could barely contain her disrespect for what she called a "ludicrous theory, if I ever heard one." She said that the crime was committed in a secured area, and the only way you could get in was with a card. She added that this was a rage crime, not a premeditated one. The person had to hide the evidence, and he did a good job. He did not just run out the door. The person definitely worked in the lab, said Brown. "This was not an outside crime. This is basically a sex crime and a body was hidden. Animal rights people leave messages." There was absolutely no chance, she said, that it was an animal rights activist.

Who was right? Only time would tell.

On CNN's news show *AC360°*, host Anderson Cooper asked Dr. Cyril Wecht, a forensic pathologist, why authorities would not release the autopsy results in the Le case. Wecht said it was a tactic of the investigation. The police would use information learned at the autopsy—information that they were withholding—to keep suspects in the dark and off-balance during interviews and interrogations. They would wait to find out what suspects, such as Clark, might have to say, before they revealed their cards. *Was Le raped? Strangled? Beaten? Was her skull fractured?* Wecht said the authorities already knew all that. But "they want to hear the story of their suspects. They want to hear what he has to say. For example, he'll say, 'You know, I really didn't do anything. We were just making out or so on and she fainted and passed out and I panicked or whatever.'" In fact, Wecht added, the police "want to find out exactly what he's going to say about all of the physical events in order to see what they can confront him with." They "want that hole to be dug before they tell [the suspect] what really happened and he fits his story with his attorney into that scenario."

According to Wecht, the Le murder was a crime of passion and "continued in a frenzied fashion." He couldn't say whether it was a planned or premeditated, but he felt that the perpetrator knew what he was doing. He did not hurriedly leave the building and draw suspicion to himself. He stayed to finish up his work.

Cooper then asked Jack Levin, a criminologist, "Did she know her killer?"

"Almost definitely," Levin responded. "Most homicides are committed over arguments. They know their victim very well. . . . Unlike an outsider, this killer stayed around and took time and a risk and looked for an effective place to conceal the body. A robber, an outsider, would want to race out. My guess is that the wedding cannot be ignored. I wouldn't be surprised if we're seeing a person who was obsessed with her." This might have been a case, Levin added, of "if I can't have her, nobody can."

DNA testing had been made the number one priority, and technicians worked from the minute they received Clark's DNA, early Wednesday morning, until late into Wednesday night.

New Haven Police chief James Lewis said, "If we have one match on a person we know was at that location," the police would arrest the person. Rumor had it that the results would be back in days, or sooner. They could not come back soon enough.

Late Wednesday night, the police called a news conference. The media and the public believed that something was about to be revealed about the lab results. At this point, it was no longer *I hope we can still find Le alive.* Rather, it was *Le is dead. Now let's get the killer!*

The police reported that indeed, some results had come back from the lab. First, they stated that the lab had looked at the green-ink pen found with Le's body in order to compare and analyze it to known DNA from the victim and Clark. The results: A bloodstain on the pen matched Le's DNA, but DNA analysis did *not* find Clark's blood on the pen. Spirits dropped. However, the authorities added, Clark's DNA *was* located on a swabbing of the interior of the pen cap and on a portion of the barrel.

This was huge.

Every day, Clark signed himself in with a pen that used green ink. It was his signature. Sign-in sheets from the day of the killing showed that Clark signed in with the green-ink pen early in the day, and then at one point, he stopped using it and switched to black ink—a complete anomaly. *Could Clark have inadvertently dropped the pen into the cavity in the wall where Le's body was concealed?* That's what the pen in the wall seemed to be saying.

According to the police, the lab also determined that Clark's DNA was on Le's body, as well as on her clothing. Again, that was huge. Since there was no evidence that Le and Clark were involved in an intimate relationship, why would DNA from Clark be on Le? The answer seemed obvious.

That evening, a tow truck hauled away Clark's red Ford Mustang from the Super 8 parking lot.

At last, it seemed, the mystery that kept people all over the world captivated was about to be solved—and it was not a pretty picture. Strangulation in itself was gruesome enough—the pain, the gasping for air, the desperate struggle to survive. But there was also blood everywhere. It was inside the wall cavity where Le was hidden, on several items of clothing, on the box of wipes, and on the walls in different basement rooms.

Something more then *simply* strangulation seemed to have taken place. But what exactly was it?

SIX

After getting back the DNA results on Wednesday evening, police planned to arrest Clark by midnight. However, when midnight came, they still had not completed the paperwork needed for the arrest warrant. As some officers worked feverishly throughout the night to fill out the paperwork, others staked out the motel where Clark was staying, monitoring the outside of his room, the stairwell, and the parking lot to make sure Clark couldn't sneak away.

By 7 a.m., Thursday morning, reporters, photographers, and curious onlookers were camped out across the street from the Super 8 Motel in Cromwell. Everyone was expecting that Raymond Clark would be arrested. Five police cars stood as sentinels in the parking lot.

A little after 8 a.m., authorities closed down the highway outside the motel and blocked the road leading into it.

At approximately 8:23 a.m. a convoy of police and FBI cars raced to the motel, sirens blaring. Police surrounded the building.

At 8:24 a.m., two plainclothes state detectives knocked on the door of the second-floor motel room, where Clark was staying with his father.

Six minutes later, Clark exited the room in handcuffs,

walked down a long hallway, and was directed into a black Mercury with tinted windows. Onlookers who had come to see what all the commotion was about burst into applause as Clark was escorted into the patrol car. Clark was wearing a white and tan striped polo shirt and tan pants.

One spectator described Clark as a "clean-cut kid, somber, head down" as he passed through the lobby. The person stated that the whole incident was "pretty uneventful." Captain Roy Nelson, a local police official on the scene, concurred. "It was a peaceful arrest."

Clark was driven to the New Haven police station. Then, just after 10 a.m., Clark was led into a courtroom at the New Haven Superior Court for his arraignment. With legs shackled, he was surrounded by eight judicial marshals. His attorney David Dworski was no longer on the case. Two public defenders, Joseph Lopez and Beth Merkin from the Connecticut Public Defender's Office, had been assigned and now stood by his side as he was taken before the judge. The courtroom was filled with journalists. None of Clark's family was present, nor were any members of Le's family.

Clark looked to be in shock during the three-minute arraignment presided over by Judge Jon C. Blue. Standing between his two public defenders, his hands on a table in front of him, and with a tattoo clearly looped around each forearm, Clark looked so meek that it didn't seem possible he could harm a mouse—not to mention a person.

Blue asked the suspect if he had been read his rights. Clark, with his head down, softly responded, "Yes, sir." Clark was then officially charged with murder.

The prosecutors requested bail to be set at $3 million. But because Clark had no prior criminal history, bail commissioner Sharon Moye-Johnson requested that the $3 million bail be reduced to $1 million, as did Clark's public defender Beth Merkin—even though, according to Moye-Johnson, Clark would not attend the prearraignment interview she always held to assess a defendant's flight risk. However, Blue refused to lower the bail, citing the "serious nature of the crime."

The issue of bail having been resolved, both Clark's public defenders and the prosecution asked that the warrant be sealed for two weeks because the investigation was ongoing. After giving it some thought, Blue complied with the attorneys' request. He set Clark's next court date for October 6.

After this brief appearance, Clark was taken to the New Haven Community Correctional Center on Whalley Avenue. Commenting on Clark's demeanor, Lieutenant John Bernard of the correctional center said, "It's his first time in jail. This is all new to him. He hasn't cried. He hasn't said a word to anyone." Bernard said that Clark was put into solitary out of fear that someone might want to harm him. "We don't know who is out there maybe waiting to take action against him," said the lieutenant.

Several hours later, Clark was transferred to the MacDougall-Walker Correctional Institution in Suffield, twenty miles north of Hartford. Described on its website as "a high/maximum security level multi-mission facility" for adult men, including those who need "pretrial protective custody," the institution "provides a highly structured environment to manage long-term sentenced offenders, protective custody offenders and high bond unsentenced offenders with programs designed to address the needs of each population."

Because neither he nor his family could even hope to raise enough money to meet the $3 million bail, Clark would remain at MacDougall-Walker Correctional for the immediate future.

Clark's arrest brought an enormous sense of relief to the Yale community—at least the killer was off the streets and off the campus—but it also raised innumerable questions. The public and the media still wanted to know exactly what evidence the authorities had against Clark. Not knowing the motive or the details of the crime made people edgy and even outraged. And before Clark's fingerprints had time to dry at the New Haven police station, attacks began to be hurled against the university and all of the police agencies involved in the case.

Many verbalized their anger about the fact that Clark was an employee of Yale in the first place. *How could the university have hired such a person?* Yale President Richard Levin released a statement saying that there was nothing in Clark's employment record that would have hinted at a capacity for such violence. "His supervisor reports that nothing in the history of his employment at the university gave an indication that his involvement in such a crime might be possible," Levin said. "This incident could have happened in any city, in any university, or in any workplace. It says more about the dark side of the human soul than it does about the extent of security measures." He assured the Yale community that Clark— should he make bail—had been banned from coming on campus and that his job had been suspended. He urged the Yale community "to resist the temptation to rush to judgment until a full and fair prosecution of this case brings a just resolution." Levin said that the New Haven police reported that they hadn't received any prior complaints about Clark. "It is frightening that a member of our own community might have committed this terrible crime. But we must not let this incident shatter our trust in one another. We must reaffirm our deepest values as an institution—our commitment to the search for truth, undertaken in a spirit of openness, tolerance, and civility."

During a news conference, Levin responded to a question about emails being sent by Clark to Le. He stated, "To my knowledge there's nothing that would be relevant to the case" in the emails between the two people.

Several students questioned what kind of background check, if any, was done on Clark before he was hired by the university. One researcher was quoted as saying that Yale had "questionable hiring practices" and wondered if "family hires" were as adequately screened as external candidates. The researcher pointed out that although Clark might not have had a criminal record, more likely than not, "he was not hired through standard hiring channels and procedures."

And then came the criticism about the amount of time it took to locate Le, whose body was found in the very building where she was last seen. *How could it have taken so long to thoroughly search the building?* It took the police from September 8 to September 13 to find her body—five full days to locate her in the building she never left. Furthermore, said many angry students, there were plenty of clues right before the authorities' eyes, if only they had looked hard enough: There was blood on two walls as well as blood on a Wipe-Alls box discovered on Wednesday. *Couldn't a hundred investigators have done a better job of searching the lab?* Some took to calling the police the "Keystone Kops."

After the arrest, Natalie Powers, Le's roommate, told the New York *Daily News,* "He is a monster. He killed my roommate. He left her in a wall. How am I supposed to feel? I feel sick. I don't care what happens to him at this point so long as he can no longer hurt anyone else."

On Thursday night, September 17, two of Clark's old friends appeared on CNN's *Larry King Live*. They were Bobby Heslin, who was identified as the accused's "best friend, who grew up next door to Clark" in Branford, and Maurice Perry, a "childhood friend of Clark since the first grade." King began by asking Heslin his reaction to the arrest of his buddy. Heslin said he was completely shocked that Clark was a murder suspect because "that's not the Raymond Clark who I have known my whole entire life." Perry stated that he, too, was stunned and right now, "I can't say that I believe he's guilty. I mean I've known him so long I just can't picture him doing something like this." Heslin added that it was unreal to turn on the TV and to see the best friend who had walked with him to the bus stop every day and waited with him "for that Bus Number 11" to be accused of something like this.

Then King brought *New Haven Independent* reporter Marcia Chambers into the discussion. Chambers described an alleged incident in 2003 at Branford High School with Clark's then girlfriend, in which she went to police to report that Clark "forced her to have sex with him." Afterward, the reporter stated, the detectives called Clark's parents to alert them to the situation. When King asked Clark's two buddies if they knew anything about this, both Heslin and Perry said that they had never heard anything about it. Nor, they admitted, did they know he was currently engaged, though Heslin knew he had a girlfriend.

King then called on Dr. Michael Welner, an associate professor of psychiatry at New York University's School of Medicine, who was the developer of the "Depravity

Scale" (a measurement based on forensic evidence, that denotes what aspects of a given crime were depraved and the degree of a specific crime's depravity—created in an attempt to enhance fairness in sentencing). King asked Welner to weigh in on what the two friends had just said. Welner noted that it was not unusual for friends to keep secrets from friends. To him, what *was* important was that Clark had friends; that he was gainfully and steadily employed; that he was not in a particular crisis at the present time; and that he was loved by a woman whom he was going to marry. When King asked, "So what do you make of this, then?" Welner said he believed more would come out about the story and he felt that forensic pathology (a subspecialty of forensic medicine which deals with the cause and manner of death) would emerge as the key tool to discovering what actually happened. And he added that, by far, in the workplace, "the most common cause of a homicide of a male toward a female is rejection."

After a break, King was joined by Judge Jeanine Pirro, host of the TV show *Judge Pirro* and a former district attorney, along with well-known defense attorney Michael Cardoza. King asked Pirro what she felt after hearing Clark's friends speak from their heart about their good friend. Pirro responded, "Nobody really knows what a murderer is like. I mean, people don't show that side of themselves." Cardoza posited that Clark would probably have a tough time at trial because "I think most people listening right now probably have him convicted."

Before King went on to discuss another "sensational crime," both Perry and Heslin said that they would try to contact their friend Raymond Clark. "I will definitely send him a letter. I have always wanted to catch up with him," said Perry. But, he added, he wished it was under happier circumstances and that something other than Ray's arrest had inspired him to reach out to his old friend.

At a late press conference that night, Yale Police chief James Perrotti said, "The Yale community is grateful for the collaborative efforts of the New Haven Police, the state police, and the FBI, and for their tireless devotion over the last eight days to the difficult task of finding Annie Le and determining who is responsible for this horrible crime." Pastor Dennis Smith, spokesperson for the Le family, said that the arrest is "wonderful news" and will go a long way to helping the family begin to find closure. "It's such a terrible thing to have lost Annie," he said.

That night, Ngoc-Tuyet Bui, the aunt who raised Le in Placerville, sent an email to family and friends, asking them to pray for her. A grieving James Bui, Le's uncle, sent an email thanking the public for their "support and prayers in our time of grief. That is the only statement we can make right now."

The Widawsky family issued a statement thanking everyone who was involved in preparations "for a wedding that was not to be." They added, "Our lives have been a whirlwind from the moment we first knew that Annie [was] missing. We share in the grief of the family of Annie Le and are, collectively, doing our best to deal with our tragic loss. Annie will be in our hearts forever."

Late that night, a red Ford Taurus was seized by the police, although it was not clear what the police hoped to find in the car or who the car belonged to.

SEVEN

The minute Raymond Clark was arrested for the murder of Annie Le, everyone from friends to psychiatrists to criminologists weighed in on what they believed the motive to be, tossing around their ideas like confetti—or blood spatter.

New Haven Police chief James Lewis was among the first to express his point of view: "It is important to note that this is not about urban crime, university crime, domestic crime, but an issue of workplace violence, which is becoming a growing concern around the country." He added that he would not rule out handing Clark additional charges.

This view was echoed by many others, including several people who worked in the lab with both Le and Clark. They told police that Clark viewed the research lab as his "fiefdom." They reported that Clark felt Le was flaunting the lab rules. News articles stated that Clark sent an email to Le on the day she went missing concerning the cleanliness of her mouse cages, which were under his care, and requesting a meeting with her that morning to discuss the situation. Reportedly, Clark complained that Le didn't keep her cages clean enough. According to anonymous sources, Le wrote back, in a conciliatory manner. Everyone who knew Le remarked that Le would never demean Clark or seek to put him in his place. If she was not keeping her cages up to snuff, some theorized that she may have been distracted by her upcoming wedding.

Hector Alvarez, a workplace violence prevention specialist, told ABC-News10 that most likely, Clark's behavior "didn't just start the day he allegedly killed Le." Alvarez said that a person who suffers from workplace-related anger "will allow their emotions to escalate until they reach a boiling point." Although many people believed that even if Clark had killed Le, it could *not possibly* have been over something as *minor* as mouse cage cleanliness, Alvarez pointed out that it makes no difference how seemingly important or unimportant the problem is to an outsider. The perpetrator, he stated, "still feels that frustration."

According to statistics, approximately 1,000 murders per year are due to workplace violence—a small percentage considering that over 150 million people work in the United States. However, most homicides in the workplace involve robberies, with service and retail workers being killed by strangers, not by their co-workers. Even if the number of workplace homicides seems relatively low, it is still more than one a day. And the incidence of workplace violence *excluding* murder is much higher.

Workplace violence can be triggered by a variety of events: dissatisfaction with one's boss or co-worker; unrequited romantic interest; jealousy over someone else getting a promotion; anger over workplace rules. Stephen Ross, a Fort Wayne forensic psychologist, said, "We have become a very retributive society. If someone doesn't give us what we want, we will take matters into our own hands."

* * *

Another widely discussed motive for Le's killing was that she was the victim of a gender-based crime—an offense against a woman. Gender-based violence—in its extreme—includes rape, murder, domestic violence, sexual abuse, and even forced prostitution. People who put forth this gender-based theory noted that women's lives and well-being were often in peril as they suffered from on-the-job harassment and other injustices. Such issues were not limited to the United States. In certain countries, women are flogged for wearing pants; sold into sexual slavery; raped in civil conflicts; and suffer severe psychological and physical abuse on a daily basis.

Addressing the issue of violence against women, U.S. senator Christopher Dodd spoke about the Le murder on September 25, 2009. "Unfortunately, violence against women on college campuses occurs far too often," he said. In light of the recent tragedy on Yale's campus, he was offering a grant to Yale University and Connecticut College to create programs to prevent such gender-based violence. "This funding underscores the importance of preventing violence against women at home, at the workplace, and on our college campuses. It is my hope that with these funds, education and prevention partnerships will work toward eliminating violence against women."

Statistics showed that even within the category of workplace violence, women were disproportionately affected. According to the United States Department of Labor Bureau of Statistics, 2008, "Women were identified as more likely to be a victim of homicide [than males] in the workplace."

Laura Smith, president of Yale University's union for clerical and technical workers, UNITE HERE, Local

34, of which Clark was a member, spoke about the issue at a press conference: "We are especially concerned by this tragedy because it is not just a question of security at Yale or safety in New Haven. It also is a question of the violence against women that is pervasive in this world. This crime reminds us that women are not safe."

Anna Parks, a graduate of Calhoun College, one of the twelve residential colleges at Yale, wrote a letter to the *Yale Daily News* reminding people that the Le murder was "but one tragic example of the continued victimization of women around the world." She stated that the murder was unspeakably heinous and evil, but that other attacks against women, though more subtle and less covered by the press, can also be damaging. She cited the "Pre-season Scouting Report," an email sent out by Yale men rating the attractiveness of Yale freshmen girls. Although the writer stated she in no way "equated such an email with Le's murder, both attacks contributed to an unwelcoming and unsafe climate for women on Yale's campus. Whether sexual in nature or not, any act that objectifies women decreases the value of and respect for a female life. And it paves the way for dehumanizing acts that rob us of friends, daughters and fiancées."

Criminologist Jack Levin, a professor of sociology and criminology at Northeastern University in Boston and considered an authority on hate crimes, mass murders, and serial killers, offered his opinion on ABC News on why Le was murdered. People underestimate "a killer's excessive need for power, dominance, and control." One way to satisfy an overwhelming need for control, according to Levin, "is to regain a sense of power by squeezing the life out of a happy, successful co-worker." Too often, Levin said, people automatically think that the motives for murder are jealousy, revenge, and money.

Delving even deeper into the crime, Levin spoke about the way in which Le was murdered. When one strangles another person, he said, the strangler not only demonstrates a volatile personality but control issues as well. An up-close and personal murder requires a tremendous amount of anger. "Controlling men often display their anger in their relationships with women. . . . They want to make their victims suffer or to play God by deciding who lives and who dies. There are certain men who treat their women like possessions. They may be very jealous, possessive, and feel if I can't have her, nobody can."

On *GMA Weekend*, Brad Garett, a former FBI agent and an ABC news consultant, also talked about strangulation and what it revealed about a murderer. Killing another person and strangling them, he said, "is a very personal thing because they are actually looking at you as they are doing it. Think about what anger and rage anyone would have to have."

Another theory put forth was that of unrequited love. Some people opined that Clark had secretly lusted after Le, and now that her marriage was approaching, he was outraged that he couldn't "have" her. Others went so far as to suggest that perhaps Clark and Le were involved in a romantic relationship and, at one point, she may have told him "after the wedding, we won't be able to do this anymore," so Clark "just snapped in a jealous rage."

One of Clark's former neighbors who appeared on ABC News' *Good Morning America* reinforced the idea that Clark had a "menacing" relationship with women. Ann Marie Goodwin, who lived below Clark in New

Haven before Clark moved to Middletown, stated Clark was "very controlling of his fiancée. He wouldn't let her talk to me or anything." Goodwin said Clark always walked in front of Hromadka and never opened a door for her.

Another hypothesis regarding the murder of Le was that it was a racially motivated hate killing. Supporting this premise, one writer complained that the "New Haven Police Department is suspiciously dragging its feet in arresting the primary 'white' suspect in the case. Annie Le's parents are Vietnamese immigrants and it is no secret that many white people still hold a deep hate towards that group ever since the Vietnam War."

The Asian-Nation, an online site, reported, "The last 20 years or so have seen Asian Americans become the fastest-growing targets for hate crimes and violence. Combined with the cultural stereotype of Asian Americans as quiet, weak, and powerless, more and more Asian Americans are victimized. . . ." Citing the "1999 Audit of Violence Against Asian Pacific Americans" published by the National Asian Pacific American Legal Consortium, the site noted that there was a "13 percent increase of reported anti-Asian incidents between 1998 and 1999."

Some followers of the crime were quick to point out that Clark was in the Asian Awareness Club in high school—at least he was photographed for his high school yearbook as being a member—so perhaps he had "a thing" for Asian women. Some thought it could be "yellow fever." According to the *Urban Dictionary,* "yellow fever" was a "term usually applied to white males who have a clear sexual preference for women of Asian descent, although it can also be used in reference to white females who prefer Asian men." One online commenter wrote that Clark's *not* having an Asian girlfriend may have "caused him to be even more infatuated with someone like Annie. . . . I have a feeling that he knew this was the last chance that he could have to get with Annie before she got married and felt compelled to force sex upon her, only to end up strangling her as she resisted. . . ."

On *Larry King Live*, Dr. Michael Welner put forth a theory that many other people had also been thinking about: "What if they test [Clark] and find steroids in his system and find that he had an explosive reaction and didn't know his own rage or strength with a 4'11" woman?" According to friends, Clark had looked much beefier lately. Had he been abusing steroids? Was his killing of Le induced by 'roid rage? Clark was a bully, said proponents of this theory, and "bullies are physically aggressive with hair-trigger tempers and fragile egos."

The term "'roid rage" was applied to people, most often athletes, who acted extremely aggressively or hostilely after regularly taking large doses of anabolic steroids. According to Dr. Gary I. Wadler, clinical associate professor of medicine at New York University's medical school and an expert on drug use in sports, including the phenomenon of 'roid rage, 'roid rage is a loss of impulse control, which provokes overreactions. Wadler admitted that there was no good data on how common it is, but he stated that 'roid rage had been implicated in a number of murders, most famously, pro wrestler Chris Benoit's killing of his wife and son and his hanging himself. "A lot of prescription medication was found in the home, including anabolic steroids," said Fayette County sheriff Lieutenant Tommy Pope.

David L. Katz, lawyer and psychiatrist at Harvard

Medical School, reported, "In the last seven years, at least twenty killings have been committed by men who said they had used steroids."

Another theory was that Clark suffered from Intermittent Explosive Disorder, an imbalance of brain chemistry in which a person gets angry "out of proportion" to a stress trigger. According to an article by "Dr. Chuck of Wellsphere.com," intermittent explosive disorder, or IED, "affects roughly 16 million Americans . . . and [may be] triggered by abnormal serotonin activities." Dr. Chuck stated that IED typically started at puberty, and the likelihood that Clark had some "temper outburst history in his high school years is very high. If left undetected," he added, "IED [can] have serious consequences and could lead to cold-blooded aggression." According to the Mayo Clinic website, IED can include road rage, domestic abuse, or other angry outbursts or temper tantrums. This disorder, it stated, "most often occurs in young men and may affect as many as one in 14 U.S. adults." According to the staff of the Mayo Clinic, the explosive eruptions usually span a ten- to twenty-minute timeframe. They can result in injuries and property destruction. They may occur in clusters, or they can be separated by months of nonaggression. Most often, people with IED grew up in families in which explosive behavior and physical and verbal abuse were everpresent. According to the clinic, there may be a genetic component involved in this disorder, with genes passing from parent to child.

Several sociologists conjectured that "relative deprivation" could explain Clark's actions. Relative deprivation is defined as the discontent that people experience when they feel they are being deprived of something they are entitled to—something that another person or group possesses. Criminologist Jack Levin, speaking to ABC News, stated that the mindset of a person experiencing feelings of relative deprivation could be triggered "when you are measuring your own self-worth against others and you come out on the bottom." Perhaps Clark misinterpreted Le's distracted behavior (not paying him as much attention as he wanted) for dismissiveness—and that was hard for him to take coming from a younger, smarter, and smaller woman. Ivy League Yale is composed of students with multiple degrees who are on a fast track to a productive and financially secure life. Clark, on the other hand, was cleaning animal cages and the floors of a basement lab. The gulf between the two worlds, said Levin, can lead to great tension. Clearly underlying this theory was a socioeconomic motive, with the disparity between the lifestyles and environments of Le and Clark being proposed as the primary cause for Clark's rage.

Another possible motive was put forward by those who felt Clark was enraged by the relative uncleanliness of Le's mouse cages. They felt that Clark was angered not only because the quality of Le's mouse-housekeeping was not up to his standards, causing his "fiefdom" to be less than spic and span, but also because dirty cages meant Clark had a lot of extra clean-up work to do. Records revealed that Clark sent Le an e-mail asking her to meet with him regarding the cleanliness of her mouse cages. Although, according to several researchers, it was not unusual for a tech to reprimand a researcher about lab rules, Clark might have taken this to a horrifying new level.

And then there was the surprising psycho-sexual motive suggested by Dr. Susan Block, who was "once a young Yalie" herself, and was currently a sex educator, cable TV and radio personality, author of *The 10 Commandments of Pleasure,* and founder of the Susan Block Institute for the Erotic Arts & Sciences in Los Angeles (a.k.a. Dr. Suzy's Speakeasy). She was perhaps best known for her HBO specials and for her "ethical hedonistic" view of sex. In an article titled "Of Mice and Men: The Murder of Annie Le," Block stated that one obvious theory of Le's murder was that it was a crime of passion. However, she quickly ruled that out because there were "no signs of sex or attempted sex and the suspect was already romantically involved with his own fiancée." Block then posited another theory, which she strongly believed could be the right one. She recalled that a caller telephoned her radio show several years ago and asked her for "dating advice." The person, like Clark, worked in a research lab tending to the mice. Although it was a lonely job, the caller said, he took great pride in his work—as did Clark. When Block had the caller return to the subject of dating and how he was satisfying his sexual needs, the caller stated that he satisfied himself by masturbating several times a day. And then, he blurted out, "I do it with the mice. I stick a cardboard tube up my rear and let the rats run up the tube in and out of my rectum. It feels incredible and I usually come in an instant."

The airwaves went quiet—for a second. Block managed to stay calm and react in a civilized manner, but immediately after the show, she did some research. She learned that this sort of behavior had a label. It was called "feltching" according to the *Urban Dictionary.* Block wondered if Clark—like the caller—might have been involved in feltching. Perhaps, Block posited, if Le "had caught Clark with his pants down, literally, in the lab. . . . Maybe Le had just discovered Clark's shameful secret. . . ." And he killed Le to keep his feltching secret from getting out.

Then, in what many thought was an unfair and even despicable premise, in that it slurred the deceased, a student who had attended University of Rochester with Le put forth this theory on the Internet: It was Le's arrogant and obnoxious personality that may have driven Clark over the edge. The writer stated that at Rochester, Le was "always condescending to lab personnel." She said that Le's motto was "get them before they got you. She was really manipulative and street tough." The person signed the note: "Known Annie for three years while undergraduate."

After posting her thoughts, the writer received many forwarded links to websites discussing Le and each of them ended with something like, "pray for her, she was so kind, beautiful, and smart. . . ."

"I'll tell you the truth about Annie," the naysayer wrote back. "She was nowhere NEAR as perfect as the media sources describe her. . . . She was the genius brown-noser. . . . She had an extremely calculating personality. She always had a big smile to mask everything." This person's theory was that Annie probably got on this lab tech's bad side. "The lab tech probably had an unstanble [*sic*] personality and maybe this is why he killed her."

Responses to the writer's comments were so vitriolic that the letter was ultimately taken off the Internet.

Amid all the speculating and theorizing, lawyer and legal analyst Lisa Bloom, who appeared on CBS's *The Early Show* on Friday, September 18, weighed in. She stated that although there were many possible theories, during a trial, prosecutors do not have to *prove* motive. "It's not an element of murder or any homicide crime," she said. "Sure, they'd *like* to have it, because a jury is always going to be curious as to what the motive is. But when there's a mountain of physical evidence, which sounds like what we're gathering here now, they certainly don't need to have motive."

Chief of Police James Lewis concurred. "The only person that really, truly knows the motive in this crime is the suspect. What made him do what he did, we may not know until trial. We may never know."

That may have been true, but it didn't stop people from speculating. It was human nature to want to make sense of a senseless killing. *There* had *to be a reason, didn't there?*

PART
III

ONE

With Clark's arrest on September 17—four days after the discovery of Annie Le's body—a new and even more frenetic media blitz took place. Headlines appeared in newspapers from Pottsdam, Pennsylvania, to Lubbock, Texas, and from London, England, to Bangkok, Thailand.

The headline in the New York *Daily News* read "Mouse Man Played Ball as Cops Closed In."

The *Yale Daily News* took a more sober, journalistic approach: "Clark Charged in Le GRD '13 Murder."

The *Daily Mail* in the United Kingdom wrote, "Annie Le: FBI storm lab technician's flat and take him away in handcuffs over Yale grad student's murder."

Whether he was a "mouse man" or a "lab technician," or whether police searched his "flat" or his "apartment," Clark's arrest made international news. Le's murder resonated with people everywhere. The case was spellbinding, bizarre, and seemingly inscrutable. There were so many contradictions, first among them being the striking differences between Le and Clark.

For example:

He was a muscular 5'9", 190 pounds. She was a diminutive 4'11", 90 pounds.

She was a brilliant Yale graduate student, studying

enzymes. He was a high school graduate who tended to rodents.

He cleaned floors in a lab. She was a person who hoped to help people who suffered from cancer and other diseases.

Then there were the poignant and cruel ironies of the murder:

Le had recently written an article about how Yale students could *avoid* becoming crime victims, only to become the victim of a deadly crime herself.

The prestigious university building where Le worked was riddled with security measures—electronic key cards and surveillance cameras trained on the entrances. But all this security did nothing to protect Le from her assailant.

Le was poised to prolong people's lives through breakthrough scientific discoveries, yet her own life ended so young.

Le was supposed to be married on September 13, 2009. Instead, her body was found that day stuffed in a basement wall.

On September 18, 2009, she should have been on her honeymoon in Greece. Instead that was the day her casket was brought home to California.

Life at the Amistad lab, although certainly not back to normal, was beginning to get back into a routine. The building had been reopened to all researchers, staff, and technicians on Wednesday, September 16, three days after Le's remains were found. Soon after, Amistad was once again a bustling place with serious-minded students focused on important work. However, many young researchers reported that the mood in the building was not the same. Before Le went missing, it had been a place of hopeful expectations; now it was one of sobering sadness. "It's all-consuming work, so in a way it helps, because we have to get on with our research and that, in a way, is therapeutic," said Salman Kahn, who was doing postdoctoral studies in vascular biology. "At the same time," he added, "I think there are a lot of unresolved issues."

Security guards continued to patrol the area outside of Amistad. News crews positioned themselves for another day of filming the medical school campus. They were hoping to catch any news conference or public utterance concerning Raymond Clark's arrest or the results of the DNA testing. TV reporters aired interviews with students throughout the day. To a person, all the students reported that they were relieved by the arrest, but overwhelmed with grief.

Anton Bennett, associate professor of pharmacology and thesis adviser to Le, published this statement:

In the midst of this horrific tragedy, we reach down into the depths of our hearts, to express our deepest sympathies to the family of Annie Le for their loss. To the family of Jonathan Widawsky, we also extend our greatest sympathy. Annie Le will always be remembered as a person that exuded life. Annie Le was a diligent and incredibly hard working student who showed a passion for science and the desire to make a difference in people's lives. We mourn the loss of Annie Le. We have witnessed a bright light of enormous potential prematurely extinguished—we feel sadness.

As scientists, our passion for discovery emanates from many different sources. The tragic loss of Annie Le, who had become an integral member of our laboratory, now seeds another source of inspiration. Annie Le's work will continue. We will draw

*upon the energy of Annie Le's life to help us fulfill
our efforts of striving to make a difference in this
world. We thank the Yale community, the pharmacology department, graduate students, and our
many colleagues for their support during these
difficult times.*

By day's end, the piranhaic media as well as all
those following the case on campus were given more
news concerning the DNA findings. An official, speaking on condition of anonymity, revealed that further results from DNA testing showed that Clark's DNA was
located in a ceiling tile as well as in the wall recess
where Le's body was located. The official confirmed
that in several places on lab walls, blood spatter had
been wiped off, seemingly in an attempt to hide it. The
source also reported that Clark had been seen trying to
hide equipment that had blood spatter on it.

It appeared that the noose around Clark's neck was
tightening.

Later that evening, in an exclusive interview by
News10-ABC, Le's brother Chris said that the extensive
media coverage of his sister's death had "been difficult
for his family to handle." He said that all the attention
on her death and on the arrest of a suspect "has been
overwhelming at times. We just want the media to respect our privacy. We have a lot of stuff to do. This
makes it all the much harder." He went on to say, "She
lived a good life. We want to respect that and have others respect that as well."

By nightfall, candles and flowers overflowed the entrance to the park across from 10 Amistad.

TWO

Late that Friday night, September 18, Le took her final trip home to Placerville. It was not the way it was supposed to be. Her body was accompanied by somber members of her extended family who, instead of witnessing a vibrant, loving Annie, were escorting a silent corpse.

In New Haven, Pastor Dennis Smith, spokesperson for the Le family, said that the family had asked "everyone to continue to pray for Annie and respect the family's privacy at this time." He said that the family would like any donations people wished to make in honor of Annie to go to the "I Have a Dream" Foundation, one of the two charities that Le and Widawsky had selected for their wedding registry.

Even in this time of unspeakable grief, the Le family found a way to be both generous and gracious.

That evening, Dr. Phil (i.e., Phil McGraw, the TV personality), hosted CNN's *Larry King Live* and, just as in the previous show, many guests weighed in on the Le murder. First up was Randi Kaye, Emmy Award–winning anchor and correspondent for CNN/US, based in New York City, who spoke of how Clark had piqued the interest of the police early on. According to her source, Kaye stated, Clark was seen on the video surveillance after the fire drill and he clearly stood out "with his head in his hands looking distraught." She believed he might have even pulled the alarm. The same source, Kaye said, stated that Clark's DNA clearly connected him with the victim—the victim's DNA was found on Clark. Kaye added that some media reports stated that Clark had emailed Le the day of the murder about the condition of her cages.

Thomas Kaplan, editor-in-chief of the *Yale Daily News,* was called on next. He stated that according to police reports, there was no evidence whatsoever of a romantic relationship between the two. He acknowledged that they must have had some contact in the lab, but he didn't know exactly what kind of professional relationship it was.

Criminal profiler Pat Brown was interviewed next and immediately shot down the theory that was being suggested—most vocally by Yale University and police—that the crime was an incidence of workplace violence. Brown felt it was a "silly concept" to call it workplace violence. Yes, it occurred in the workplace, said Brown, but does the crime of someone shooting another in a courtroom become a case of "courtroom violence"? Does an ex-husband who shoots his wife in the park become a case of "park violence"?

Clearly, Brown stated, this was the case of violence against a woman. Brown pointed out that Clark's high school girlfriend reported that Clark forced her to have sex with him and wouldn't let her get out of the relationship when she wanted. "What kind of man is that?" Brown wondered. "Certainly not someone with great empathy. This is scary behavior."

Perhaps, offered Brown, Clark had an obsession with Le. Maybe she didn't give him the time of day and that ticked him off. "Now, he realizes she will soon go off with another man and he'll never have her." According to Brown, Clark felt rejection, even though, from a more "normal" person's point of view, *of course* she wouldn't be interested in him—their interests and position in life are *so* different. Brown equated Clark's interest in Le to that of a fifty-year-old man with a huge gut sitting in a bar and making a pass at a gorgeous twenty-year-old. The older man gets enraged when the younger woman blows him off—unable to see the ridiculousness of the situation. Brown felt that Clark may have been very pissed off that Le was ruining his fantasy of having her by choosing another man and soon becoming his wife. According to Brown, Clark was lusting after Le. Otherwise, Brown wondered, why her? Why now?

It was interesting, Brown added, that Clark joined the Asian Awareness Club in high school. "Why?" she wondered. Perhaps it was to look for women. Many American guys, she said, think American women are too tough and that Asian women are easier to control—"smaller packages." Brown said it was her guess that Clark did have a thing for Le and wanted to control her and when he found out he couldn't, he got angry. "It is not a coincidence that she is getting married. He is a stalker type. He keeps fantasizing about her. He's not of the same level. He thinks, She is rejecting me."

Maybe Clark was frustrated, said Dr. Phil. He was running out of ways to get her—and running out of time, with her upcoming marriage.

Casey Jordan, criminologist and attorney from New York, was interviewed next. Jordan also believed that the crime was way more complex than workplace violence. She felt that Clark suffered from deep insecurities. After all, his job at Yale was only a notch above a custodian's and certainly there was a hierarchy at Yale. She stated that Clark started out working in the washroom, cleaning out cages and moving forty-pound bags of food. Obviously, there was a huge dichotomy between Le's scientific work and Clark's janitorial work, and Clark needed to overcome the differences.

Dr. Phil pointed out that in every work environment, there is a hierarchy, but in most cases, people don't act like Clark did. Sure, he was the low man on the totem pole and felt resentment at being so far down the chain, but what caused *him* to snap? wondered Dr. Phil.

Jordan said that there had to have been a variable and she felt it could have been a romantic interest. Or perhaps he was trying to prove himself as smart as she, and she didn't acknowledge him. Maybe she didn't notice him or maybe she criticized him in some way. All these could have made him enraged.

Plus, Jordan added, if anything went wrong in the lab, it was the lab tech who paid for it, so Clark could have been angered at how Le kept her cages. So, said Jordan, if you mix his controlling personality and the stressful working conditions, and if you add that he had a romantic interest in her—that could account for it.

Brown believed that wherever Clark worked, he would have had issues, since he needed people to respect him and to be in control. He may have set up a confrontation so he could tell Le where she was wrong; so she could say he was right. He wanted to make her "beg and grovel." Maybe she wouldn't say he was smart and right. According to Brown, if he couldn't get what he wanted, he would destroy it. When Le wouldn't grovel, Clark flew into a rage. He knew he wasn't going to get his prize. Le may have simply been wondering what all this was about. *What was he talking about, anyway?* Brown said that when murder is done by strangulation, the murderer looks into the person's eyes and the other person looks back. The murderer is God. He is in full control. That is just what Clark wanted, according to Brown.

Dr. Phil brought up the fact that Clark was the star quarterback and pitcher in high school. He was in leadership roles, getting plenty of strokes from coaches and teammates and students. So, Dr. Phil wondered, was Clark *really* insecure? Casey Jordan suggested that no one really knows what goes on underneath someone else's skin. Jordan felt that Clark had huge insecurities: Allegedly, he stalked his girlfriend, forced her to have sex with him, and police had to warn him to stay away from her. "It's a classic case of 'If I can't have her, no one should be able to have her.'" Further, suggested Jordan, if Clark was such a leader, why didn't he go on to college? Why did he have to use nepotism to get a lab position? Obviously, the only thing he thought he could control was his work—"nothing else was gelling for him."

When Dr. Phil called on forensic scientist Dr. Henry Lee to tell about the scratches and bruises on Clark, Lee said that Le fought back, as evidenced by the defensive wounds on Clark's body. "Her DNA was on his shoes. His DNA was on her clothing in the ceiling tile. This is extremely important. The linkage." Also, he added, the finding of a bead belonging to her necklace "is a clear indication of a violent struggle." Obviously, he added, Clark cannot control his anger.

Editor Kaplan ended the segment by saying that the mood on campus was one of relief. Although no one wanted to convict Clark before a trial, he said, people were relieved that someone who looked like the likely murderer was under arrest.

THREE

On Monday, September 21, an alarming—and gut-wrenching—article appeared in the *New York Post*. "Bride's Body Mashed," screamed the headline. The article reported that Clark had broken Le's bones in order to fit her body into the small space in the wall where she was found. Once the story hit the Internet, "broken bones" appeared everywhere:

"Her body was mangled."

"It was smashed into the wall with broken bones."

"She was like mush—she was so smashed up you couldn't recognize her."

"Accused murderer Ray Clark was so desperate to hide his heinous handiwork that he allegedly broke the bones and mangled the body . . ."

"I've been doing this a long time and I've never seen anything like that. This guy's twisted."

"Her killer had to maneuver her body around the [vertical and horizontal water] pipes."

However, just as the rumor crescendoed, authorities countered the story, hitting the airwaves immediately with a repudiation. They stated that all the recent information about how Le's body was mangled was false: Le's bones had *not* been broken.

Tom Ullmann, chief public defender in New Haven,

was outraged at the media's reports. He said that some of the information that had recently been made public, including the story about Le's bones, could make it hard to find impartial jurors for the case. He added that there would be consequences if they discovered who was disseminating the false information. Ullmann believed that it was most likely officers in the New Haven Police Department who were leaking false information, citing the *New Haven Register*'s articles that referred to "anonymous sources at the New Haven Police Department." Ullmann stated that he sent a letter to Michael Dearington, the New Haven state's attorney, requesting an investigation into who leaked the information. If they found the source, he said, he hoped that the person or persons would be fired.

Yale secretary Linda Lorimer jumped into the fray, saying that both the regional and national media had printed articles on the Le case that relied heavily on "unidentified sources." She added that she found this practice disconcerting and problematic for people who had a sincere interest in following the story.

Joe Avery, spokesperson for the New Haven Police Department, said it was hard to figure out exactly where the information was coming from since five agencies were involved, the New Haven Police Department, Yale Police Department, Connecticut State Police, FBI, and the State's Attorney's Office. But, he added, the authorities would certainly get to the bottom of it.

In the early afternoon, New Haven Police Department chief James Lewis revealed some official, and new, information. Regarding the fire alarm that went off on the day Le went missing, he said that there was no evidence that it had anything to do with Clark or with the murder. He said that he believed the leads from the physical evidence they collected might point them in the direction of another person besides Clark, but he added, he didn't expect to arrest any other people. He also revealed that bloodhounds and other dogs had not been allowed in certain rooms of the lab because of on-going experiments involving animals. Those rooms, he said, had to be searched by hand, which hampered the investigation from proceeding as quickly as he would have liked.

Later that Monday, after having been in seclusion for days, Widawsky emerged from his parents' gray ranch-style home on Bittersweet Place in Huntington, New York. On his left ring finger, he was wearing the wedding band Le would have placed on his finger on his wedding day. The reporters camped outside his home quickly took several photos of him, and many enlarged the section showing his left hand and the wedding ring he was wearing. In many papers, it became front-page news. Widawsky's next-door neighbor Lucielle Mayer, who was to attend the wedding, told the *New York Post* when asked about the ring, "It's heartbreaking. He cares about her—it's so tragic." Mayer, who was a close and long-time friend of the family's, said she cried when she thought about the wedding band and how Widawsky must feel close to Le by wearing it.

Widawsky, his sister, and his parents left their home without speaking to reporters.

FOUR

Tuesday, September 22, was just another day on campus, except that at 5:18 p.m., if anyone was aware or had taken the time to notice, the autumnal equinox occurred. At only one of two times a year, the sun crossed the equator, making day and night of approximately equal length. This moment officially marked the beginning of autumn in the northern hemisphere.

In a statement about autumn, e. e. cummings wrote, "A wind has blown the rain away and blown the sky away and all the leaves away, and the trees stand. I think, I too, have known autumn too long." Although the words no doubt referred to the many days of autumn, its sentiment seemed particularly apt on this day: Life seemed barren indeed.

Le and Widawsky had chosen Temple Beth El in Huntington for their marriage. Now the temple would instead be the location of a far sadder event, a private memorial service for Le. The rabbi and cantor felt that the best time for the service would be during the period of the High Holy Days, which that year began at sunset on Friday, September 18, with the Jewish New Year (Rosh Hashanah), and ended with the day of atonement (Yom Kippur), beginning at sunset on September 27 and continuing until nightfall the next day. Although it is customary for Jewish people to attend services during the High Holy Days, the Widawsky family put out a statement saying that unlike in past years, they would observe the High Holy Days privately and would not attend services at Temple Beth El for the foreseeable future. According to Cantor Sandra Sherry, the family wanted to make it easier for those who were attending services at the synagogue to do so in peace, without the distraction of the voracious media.

FIVE

On Wednesday at 7 p.m., September 23, just as darkness enveloped the area, over two hundred people streamed silently into Temple Beth El in the small town where Widawsky grew up. His family had attended synagogue at Beth El for years, and it was a progressive Reform congregation, whose members were "diverse in age, ethnic background, and financial status." It was a temple proud of its inclusivity.

The attendees came to pay their respects and to say a final goodbye to the bride-to-be, who did not live long enough to become the bride she expected to be. The Widawskys, friends, Columbia students, Yale faculty and administrators, and the synagogue community poured into the pews of the temple. Many of the attendees had never met Le but wished to show their sympathy and support to the family.

Lasting a little over an hour, the service alternated traditional Hebrew prayers and songs with eulogies. Officiated by the synagogue's Rabbi Jeff Clopper, the service began with the choir singing one of Le's favorite Hebrew songs, "Eili Eili." Clopper pointed out that the song was composed decades ago by a young woman who had died tragically at age twenty-three. (The composer's name was Hannah Senesh; she had volunteered to parachute into Yugoslavia during World War II in an effort to help Jews escape the Holocaust. However, Senesh was caught and executed by the Nazis in Hungary in 1944.)

Although different versions of the lyrics are sung, the following is one of the popular ones:

Eili Eili
Shelo yigameir l'olam,
Hachol v'hayam
rishrush shel hamayim,
B'rak hashamyim
t'filat ha-adam.

O Lord, my God,
I pray that these things shall never end.
The sand and the sea,
the rush of the waters,
the crash of the heavens,
the prayer of man.

After the mournful singing, Rabbi Clopper intoned, "Oh God, we pray to have the strength to make it through this time of grief and sorrow."

Cantor Sherry, who was to have officiated at Le and Widawsky's wedding, spoke next. "Annie said about Jon, and I quote, 'I never felt this depth of love for anything or anyone. I want to make him happy all the time.' " Then, addressing Widawsky, Sherry said, "May the memory of Annie Marie Le and who she was help to bring you some semblance of peace in this imperfect world."

Lauren Widawsky, Jon's younger sister and a student at Towson University in Baltimore, spoke as tears rolled down her cheeks. "This is not easy for us. This was not the plan." Lauren told how eager she had been for Le to become part of the family and to "take her on" as a sister. She recalled the many times she and Le had taken shopping trips together and had great conversations. Brightening up at the memory of Le, she joked that she was first convinced that the couple would have been happy together when Le allowed Widawsky to cut her hair. "What girl would let Jon cut her hair?" Lauren ended by speaking haltingly and directly to Le's spirit, "We have many long days ahead, and I pray my brother can recover from your loss. You did not deserve this."

Janice Lomibao, who was to have been Le's maid of honor at the wedding and who was Le's best friend at the University of Rochester, could not attend the service, but another friend of Le's read aloud Lomibao's remarks: "Those of us who knew Annie always looked up to her. She would surprise you with candy or a pair of earrings you'd been eyeing for a long time." Lomibao's words recalled how, at the University of Rochester, Le would always think of others before herself, offering to proofread her friends' resumes and personal statements when they applied for internships or jobs. In the remarks, the speaker stated Lomibao's belief that although Le cared deeply about her friends, she was nevertheless "happiest when she was around her fiancé."

A friend of Widawsky's, Matthew Bonyak, recalled one time when he, Widawsky, and Le were freshmen at Rochester. He said that Le started a conversation with them in the lounge of her dorm. "She was simultaneously studying, shopping, and talking to us," Bonyak said. "And at the end of the night, she kissed us on our foreheads." He said she had impressed both of them with her "energy and friendliness." Bonyak said that Le was "a mouse that roared," a spunky, driven person who loved shoes and had endless love for her friends, whose needs she always put ahead of her own.

Bonyak added, "Theirs was a love to be admired." He said that they often used a phrase from singer Jason Mraz's song "Lucky," to describe their relationship: "Lucky I'm in love with my best friend." Before he requested a moment of silence, Bonyak said, "As anybody who knew her would tell you, there was only one Annie Le. She was an experience, and experiences have to be shared."

The audience remained totally silent for a long moment, experiencing Annie Le's spirit together.

SIX

On Thursday, September 24, Clark's public defenders, Joseph Lopez and Beth Merkin, filed a motion asking that the arrest warrant remain sealed for an indefinite period of time, in order to give lawyers on both sides the opportunity to review all the documents that pertained to the case thus far. They felt that unsealing the arrest warrant could irreparably damage Clark's right to an impartial jury and a fair trial. The public defenders added that a defendant's constitutional rights must take priority over the public's right to know what was contained in the arrest warrant. Lopez went on to say that keeping such records sealed is not unusual in high-profile cases. In fact, he added, it is standard practice. This is done, he said, so that the lawyers have a chance to look over all the evidence before the public and media begin to weigh in.

Clark's next court date was scheduled for October 6. On that date, Judge Roland Fasano would most likely schedule a hearing on the motion to keep the warrant sealed.

SEVEN

On Friday, September 25, the Yale Office of Public Affairs announced that a university memorial service would be held for Le on October 12 at Battell Chapel at 5 p.m. Yale also declared it was establishing a scholarship fund in Annie Le's honor.

The university also released a "Statement by the Deans of the School of Medicine and Graduate School in Memory of Annie Le," which began:

> *The Graduate School, the School of Medicine, and the entire Yale community are deeply saddened by the tragic death of graduate student Annie Marie Le, 24, on September 8. . . .*

After giving details about Le's life, the statement quoted a tribute written by members of Le's lab group:

> *Although Annie was small in size, she had a large heart and a personality that filled the room. No challenge ever seemed too large for her to overcome. Annie was a diligent and motivated student who was truly excited about her future. Annie, you are a bright and shining star, we will miss you and we will remember you always.*

The statement then quoted the words of Le's family:

Annie was loved by everyone who knew her and special to all those who came in contact with her. She was a kind-hearted human being, who was devoted to her family and friends, always sacrificing her time to help others. Her laughter was infectious and her goodness was ingenuous. . . . She was a considerate daughter, a thoughtful sister, a generous niece, a spirited cousin, a loving granddaughter, and a gracious friend. We will always remember her beautiful smile, her fun-loving spirit, and the joy that she brought to us all. Annie Marie Le will be profoundly missed.

The statement went on to mention the names of the people who survived Le, including her fiancé Jonathan Widawsky; her father and his wife, Mr. and Mrs. Hoang Le; her mother, Mrs. Vivian Van Le; her brother, Chris Tri Le; her half-siblings, Martin Le and Emmie Le; her guardian parents, Mr. and Mrs. Robert Linh Nguyen and their three children, Dan, Ryan, and Sean Khiem; her grandmother, Mrs. Thang Thi Vu; as well as aunts, uncles, and cousins.

EIGHT

Now that Le's body was in her home state, in the care of the Green Valley Mortuary, in Rescue, California, it was the grief-stricken family's somber duty to conduct a funeral service for the young woman they loved and admired.

On Saturday, September 26, around seven hundred black-clad mourners came to pay respects to Annie Le in a private mass held at the Holy Trinity Catholic Church in El Dorado Hills, in the foothills of the Sierra Nevada. The uncovered poplar casket, draped in a white cloth, was positioned in the front of the nave, the sun streaming through the windows like rays of hope.

Before the service began, over a dozen members of the media stood silently outside the church. Monsignor James Kidder, who had been Le's pastor from the time she was a young girl, recalled meeting Le for the first time. He said she was with a bunch of her friends, "and she had the biggest smile." He called Le "a rare person . . . a person who is naturally good." Kidder stated that Le was "lots of fun and she had a wicked sense of humor" and although she was always busy, she "always had time for others." He added that the Le family "is hoping this day and this ceremony will be a real moment, not just in the sense of putting Annie away, but in the sense of reconciling." Kidder then went on to reveal his personal anguish "There's a lot of mystery in this for me." In trying to come to terms with Le's death, he said, he had looked "to the center of his faith."

The service began with readings from Job, Paul, Corinthians, and Matthew, all chosen by Le's family, and read in both Vietnamese and English. From St. Matthew, the congregation read: "Blessed are those who mourn, for they shall be comforted."

Kidder then spoke. "We could ask a thousand whys for the rest of our life," he began. Then he paused before stating that the service "was a chance for the family itself to come to reconciliation with what humanly is irreconcilable: not only the fact that Annie died, but the way she died." He praised Le's dedication to medicine and her volunteer work at the Marshall Hospital where she cared for the sick. "The worth of Annie's life was not its length," he said dolefully. "It was the intensity of its love, the intensity of passion, the intensity of care." Annie "had a heart that led her to say she wanted to do the best and be the best, to keep people from having their lives cut short." Then, barely able to utter the words, he added, "Ironic, isn't it, that *her* life was cut short."

After the Eucharist, Le's mother, siblings, and maternal great-uncle offered eulogies.

Vivian Van Le, Le's mother, spoke first. She read a poem that she had written when she first heard of her daughter's death. She recited the poem in Vietnamese, and Le's brother Christopher translated it afterward. "Farewell, my child, you are here lying in the cold coffin. You were born in my loving embrace, the most wonderful gift that God had sent to me. I sang lullabies by your side this week, like I did when you were a baby, wishing you a peaceful sleep. You left life at too young an age, all of your dreams and hopes of your future gone with you to your resting place." She continued, "Now that you are gone, I will sing a different sort of lullaby." Le's mother said that her daughter's death was "like a knife searing through my soul." At the end of her reading of the poem, she addressed Widawsky, saying, "Jon, even now Annie is gone, but I still have you. I love you very much. You are my son."

Not one eye in the audience was dry.

Dan Nguyen, fifteen, considered by Le to be her younger brother, said that he loved his sister's silliness and friendliness. Whenever Le returned to Placerville, Nguyen said, Le, he, and their siblings would watch cartoons and play with stuffed animals. He added that on everyone's birthday, Le would send a present. She would talk to him as if he were still five years old—even when she was older. "It was through these little things that she did—her silliness, and friendliness, and not her academic achievement—that made the most impression on us." He said that she always brought a smile to their faces. He stated that the family was so proud of Annie's academic achievements. However, he added, "To my family, her character was more important. She was compassionate and loving." And finally, speaking to Annie herself, he said, "I miss you and I will always love you."

The last family member to speak was the uncle, or guardian, who raised Le, Robert Nguyen. He thanked everyone for coming to the ceremony and thanked people from around the country and the world for their thoughts and prayers. "Although our beloved Annie is no longer with us," he said, "she continues to live deep in our hearts as we remember her graceful smile and the fullness of life with which she lived."

Throughout the ceremony, friends and relatives broke down in tears as they listened to remembrances of the bubbly young woman who wanted to make the world a better place. Now, her dreams of healing the sick would forever be lost. Thang Thi Vu, Le's grandmother, could not keep the tissues from covering her face, as she sobbed throughout the ceremony.

Widawsky and his family attended the service, although Widawsky did not speak. Widawsky's eyes remained downcast the entire time, and he looked ghost-white and grief-stricken. His father's arm hugged him lovingly around the shoulder.

The bishop of the Diocese of Sacramento, Jaime Soto, ended the service. "We do not let cruelty or violence own the sorrow," he said, referencing the way Le died. "We let love own the sorrow. It was Annie's love for her family and friends, for her fiancé that gives us such sorrow as well as our love for her."

"Amazing Grace" was sung in both Vietnamese and in English. The service concluded with the hymn "Be Not Afraid," which played as the heartbroken mourners filed outside the church.

You shall cross the barren desert
But you shall not die of thirst
You shall wander far in safety
Though you do not know the way . . .
Be not afraid
I go before you always
Come follow Me
and I shall give you rest . . .

After the service, eight somber pallbearers wearing white gloves, white scarves, and white roses in their lapels carried Le's poplar casket to the waiting hearse, which would take her to her final resting place high on a hill in a cemetery plot facing west, nestled in the shadows of giant oak trees in Rescue. There, a private service would follow.

As Le's casket was solemnly carried to the hearse, one of the attendees said, "Her boundless spirit is what is remembered."

Former classmate Christopher Volk said that he believed that everything in life happened for a reason. But, he added, Le's death was impossible to understand. "Of all the people in the world," he wondered blankly, "why her?"

NINE

As to the haunting question of "Why her?" and "Why the crime at all?" Dr. Michael Welner, chairman of the Forensic Panel and a forensic psychiatrist who examines some of the most complex homicides in America, weighed in. He cautioned, however, that what he had to say was based *only* on the information he had read and *not* on any direct involvement in the case. He stated that he had never interviewed Clark or anyone else involved in the Annie Le case.

As to why the crime might have happened, Welner stated that by far, the most common motive for a male-female homicide is rejection. Assuming Clark was the killer, Welner could not state, without seeing more evidence, that Clark *intended* to kill Le when they met that morning. However, whatever Clark may have wanted from Le could have instigated a severe enough confrontation that he ultimately intentionally killed her.

Welner pointed out that the most common cause of workplace violence is *not* one in which a person goes "postal," referring to the violence that results from a firing or a resentful relationship with a boss. Rather, Welner stated, the most common trigger for workplace violence is the rejection of the amorous advances of a stalker. It is entirely possible that Clark was obsessed with Le and didn't have the wherewithal to express that obsession. This "silent" obsession would have played out entirely in his mind. "Inner obsession," said Welner, "can be just as intense as that which begets the endless writing and phone calls—and just as combustible. Perhaps, even, all the more so when it has no outlet."

Welner remarked that just because Clark had the outer trappings of normalcy—a gainful job, a fiancée, friends, athletic interests—these facts did not rule out a morbid fixation on Le. Obsessional attachments can absolutely happen outside of one's intimate relationship. But, Welner added, "a homicide as an endpoint is the province of a person who is so absorbed in his internal drama that he has nothing to lose. Clark had *a lot* to lose. It is for this reason," stated Welner, "that I think he killed her—because if he didn't kill her [after a violent altercation in which Le got hurt], he would indeed lose all that he had: job, fiancée, and so on."

Welner felt that the available evidence pointed most to a scenario in which Clark reacted to whatever was going on between them, and then "finished her off when it was obvious to him that he had committed a violent felony (possibly sexual) that would render him unemployable, unmarriable, and facing lengthy incarceration." But to say that *for certain* that was what took place, Welner warned he would need to know more than what was currently available to him.

From Welner's point of view—in the absence of any weapon having been found—the amount of blood on the wall in G13 *could* have been from a blow to the head, in which arteries in the scalp were impacted. Le and Clark could have had a violent struggle in which Le hit her head. The fact that Clark tried so hard to clean it all up spoke to his personality as a stickler for detail and order.

Welner pointed out that the fact that Clark's high

school girlfriend had to be escorted to and from school after, according to her, Clark forced her to have sex with him "speaks to the intensity of his fixation and to his determination. It does not make him a killer. But it does mean he is one who separates poorly, and who has a sense of entitlement about what he believes to be his."

In thinking about Clark, Welner was reminded of the movie *Everybody's All-American*, in which a star athlete is pitched into a personal crisis and troubling transition after his sports career ends. That Clark was both the quarterback and a star pitcher in high school created a pedestal of entitlement. An immature man in such circumstances often relates to women as property. Welner wondered, given this history, whether Clark's relationship to his co-workers was one of general resentment—resentment of the constant reminder of his inadequacy (relative to what he was in high school) as well as to the inescapability of his situation due to a lack of higher education and his competitive inferiority.

Welner added that without additional input, we cannot yet even be sure whether Clark was even aware of his intense attraction to Le. It is also possible that Clark played out that attraction in a more confrontational and resentful way, especially since others saw her as socially agile, confident, and popular among senior scientists. Welner also considered whether Le's Vietnamese heritage might have played a role. When he first heard about the murder, he felt that Clark's feelings about Vietnamese people in particular warranted examination over and above his reactions to other Asian peoples. The complex role of American males to presumably submissive Vietnamese females, including postwar relationships that continued in the United States, is distinct from other dynamics. "This feature pokes my curiosity for his cultural sensitivities," he commented.

When asked about the callousness of Clark playing softball six days after Le went missing—and on the day Le's body was located—Welner offered this thought: "The playing field gives him comfort and is home to him. He was coping with stress of a situation out of his control in an area where he has mastery."

Welner did not believe Clark anticipated killing Le (that he had the *intent* to kill her) in the Amistad basement because he was customarily so attentive to detail that he would have first contemplated how difficult it would be to get away with murder in that location, and then would have devised another scheme.

"I believe their *encounter* was premeditated, and his intent was illegal, but I do not believe that he saw it ending this way. He had no weapon, no means for hiding a body, and everything he reportedly did was improvisational."

TEN

The story of Annie Le's life had come to its tragic close. But bright and early the next Monday morning, the story of Raymond Clark played on, as the wheels of justice began to turn and cogitate. The media was eager for more information about the unfolding case against Clark. The arrest warrant was still sealed—and a judge wouldn't address that issue until October 6 at the earliest. But the seal on the *search* warrants was due to expire. Surely, the search warrants would contain more details about what investigators had discovered—and help explain the still-unfathomable murder.

But the expectations of those who were following the case were quashed: On September 28, Superior Court Judge Roland Fasano, following the request of both the prosecutors and the defense, stated that the multiple search warrant affidavits for Clark would remain sealed for another two weeks—until October 12.

Then, two days later, on Wednesday, September 30, Clark's public defenders requested that the judge keep the search warrant affidavits for Clark sealed *indefinitely*. Although no ruling was made on this request, the media and public were outraged. *What right do they have to keep these documents sealed? Wasn't this public information? How were Yale students, faculty, and staff supposed to feel safe if they remained in the dark about the circumstances of the crime and its investigation?*

ELEVEN

On Tuesday morning, October 6, Raymond Clark III was taken from maximum-level security prison MacDougall-Walker Correctional Institution in Suffield, Connecticut, to the Connecticut State Superior Court on Church Street. His appearance lasted less than ten minutes. Wearing handcuffs in front of him and a bright orange short-sleeved prison jumpsuit, with his tattooed forearms visible, he looked clearly frightened. Instead of wearing preppy tan pants and a striped short-sleeved T-shirt, which showed off his thick muscles, he had on regulation prison garb. Instead of sporting wavy brown hair, he had a new buzz cut.

Clark did not enter a plea and said only a few words to his two public defenders. During the brief hearing, Judge Fasano said that on October 20 the court would hear arguments regarding the sealed search and arrest warrant affidavits—and whether or not they should remain sealed indefinitely. The judge also granted the *Hartford Courant* the right to lobby to unseal the affidavits. The lawyer for the *Courant,* Paul Guggina, who worked at the law firm of Hinckley, Allen & Snyder LLP in Hartford, stated that because the case was a high-profile one, it was unreasonable to argue that unsealing the documents would taint a jury pool. He added that little was known about what was contained in the warrants, except that the results of DNA and polygraph tests pointed to Clark. (However, when the warrants were made public, no information about a polygraph test was included, even though the media reported that when Clark was given the test, the machine went off the chart when he was asked if he knew where Le was now.)

Judge Fasano added that on October 20, both sides would be able to introduce evidence and call witnesses, and from the information ascertained, he would determine whether or not there was probable cause for the case to go forward.

After the hearing, public defender Joe Lopez explained that Connecticut law stated that defendants charged with any crime punishable by death or life in prison do not have to enter a plea until a judge has determined that there is "probable cause," a reasonable belief that the person has committed the crime. Thus far, there had not been a probable cause hearing, so no probable cause had been established.

TWELVE

On October 12, a memorial service open to only the Yale community and Le's and Widawsky's families and friends took place at Yale's Battell Chapel. Around two hundred people attended. Security was tight, as all gates to the Old Campus were locked and Yale IDs were required in order to be admitted. Elegant-looking police officers, clad in dress uniforms, escorted the Le and Widawsky families to their seats. At the front of the chapel an enormous photograph of a smiling Le looked out over the congregation.

The service began with music of Johannes Brahms played on the piano by Robert Blocker, dean of the School of Music. Michelle Mo, GRD '14 in pharmacology, then played a poignant violin solo.

University Chaplain Sharon Kugler greeted the attendees before Reverend Robert Beloin, Roman Catholic Chaplain from St. Thomas More Chapel, said a prayer. President Levin lauded Le as a "model student for the Yale of the twenty-first century," and then praised the close-knit Yale community: "When one thread is pulled, the afghan unravels."

Graduate School dean Jon Butler spoke about how much Le loved science, as well as all of her friends.

The 23rd Psalm was read in Vietnamese by her

brother Dan Nguyen. The psalm was then read in English by Alexandra Teixeira GRD '14.

The Lord is my Shepherd; I shall not want.
He maketh me to lie down in green pastures:
He leadeth me beside the still waters.
He restoreth my soul:
He leadeth me in the paths of righteousness for
His name' sake.

Yea, though I walk through the valley of the
shadow of death,
I will fear no evil:
For thou art with me;
Thy rod and thy staff, they comfort me.
Thou preparest a table before me in the presence
of mine enemies;
Thou anointest my head with oil;
My cup runneth over.

Surely goodness and mercy shall follow me all
the days of my life,
and I will dwell in the House of the Lord forever.

Anton Bennett, Le's thesis advisor, spoke eloquently. "She wore her dreams for all to see. Annie was always smiling. She was happy with her life, happy with herself, and happy with her dreams." He pointed out that Le's scientific achievements were already noteworthy and that a paper she co-wrote would be published posthumously.

Bennett went on to tell some "Annieisms," remarking that when he introduced his Ph.D. students who were defending their dissertations, he traditionally began by stating some of their lab quirks. He said he would like to share some of Annie's with the audience. On one Friday, Bennett said, Le was to perform particularly messy experiments. Instead of wearing the appropriate outfit—jeans—she wore a skirt. "Today is skirt Friday," she said to him. "I always wear skirts on Friday."

Friend and fellow graduate student Tara Bancroft added a lab quirk Annieism of her own. She said that she was in awe at how her petite friend could "wear five-inch heels while doing laborious mouse surgeries, eat fried chicken and not gain a pound, and use smiley faces in her presentations and not lose respect." She also spoke of how Annie would excuse herself in the middle of a discussion she was having with friends to get a pedicure. Bancroft prayed that Annie Le would find an afterlife in which "designer handbags are plentiful, there's a Popeye's on every corner, and there are no diseases for you to spend your life trying to cure." She ended by saying that Le's outside beauty was no match for her inner beauty.

THIRTEEN

Raymond Clark entered Judge Fasano's New Haven courtroom on October 20 with a blank expression on his face. He took baby steps, encumbered by heavy leg shackles and surrounded by four judicial marshals. His hands were cuffed in front of him, and he bit his lower lip.

Throughout the forty-five-minute proceedings, Judge Fasano heard arguments from media lawyer Paul Guggina on one side, and the defense and prosecution on the other, as to whether or not the case's arrest and search warrant affidavits should remain sealed. Guggina was now not only representing the *Hartford Courant*, but also the Associated Press, the *New York Times*, and the *New Haven Register*. As the debate wore on, Clark sat stone still, staring directly at the judge but saying nothing.

Paul Guggina strongly requested that the documents be unsealed. He stated that because there had been so much nationwide attention to the case and because the case involved, among other issues, workplace violence and safety on college campuses, the public had a right to know what was contained in the documents. Furthermore, he argued, so much information had already been leaked—including that Clark failed a lie-detector test, that he was in various rooms in the lab the day of the murder, and that his DNA was found in the basement lab—that releasing the documents would either prove this information was correct or prove it false. "It does a disservice to the jury process," he noted, "to suggest that it would be impossible [for a juror who followed the case in the newspaper] to be objective about a case." He believed that the public had a First Amendment right to the information, which, in his opinion, overrode protecting a defendant's right to a fair trial.

Further supporting his case, Guggina noted that under Connecticut's unique trial system, attorneys were permitted to question prospective jurors individually for as much time as they wished, which in his mind meant that people who had already formed an opinion about the case could be weeded out. He said, "It's up to the jury to decide. A jury can make a decision based on evidence presented at the trial."

Clark's lawyers argued that the documents should remain sealed "to ensure that [our] client, Mr. Clark, receives a fair trial" and will be judged by "a jury that is not affected by negative pretrial publicity." Prosecutor John Waddock stated that the grief the Le family felt—not only because their beloved daughter was dead but also because her body was discovered on the day she was to be married—was reason enough to spare the family more agony. He added that the Le family was "deeply concerned that releasing any information about their loved one's death will invade their privacy right," thus making "this difficult time much more difficult."

After listening to both sides, Judge Fasano stated that the seal would remain in place until he was ready to make his decision on the issue.

Then, speaking to the issue of probable cause, Judge Fasano set a date of November 3 for a hearing. At that time, he said, the prosecution was to offer evidence showing probable cause for the murder charge. After that, he, the judge, would decide whether or not the state had enough evidence to go to trial. By law, a probable cause hearing must take place within sixty days of an arrest, which in Clark's case, would be by November 17—unless the court could show good cause as to why an extension was necessary.

After a silent Clark was led out, the court proceedings were over. Several lawyers immediately weighed in on the day's events. Some stated that because it was highly unusual for a family to be involved in the issue of whether or not to keep documents sealed, the judge would probably take their point of view under serious consideration.

Other lawyers disagreed, stating that most documents do not remained sealed for lengthy periods, and they predicted that the documents would soon be released. Some felt that this was a freedom of the press issue. Warrants were usually public documents, they argued, but in this case, the courts had ruled to seal them—twice. Surely, they felt, this could not go on forever.

After the hearing, Joe Lopez stated that his client would eventually give a "pro forma plea of not guilty." Beth Merkin explained that in murder cases, a plea is not entered until after one of two things occurred: after a probable cause hearing was conducted and probable cause was found; or after the right to a probable cause hearing was waived.

According to Lopez, the standard was extremely low for proving probable cause. But observers less sympathetic to Clark commented that, in this case, the standard wouldn't need to be low. Although the warrants containing details of the investigation were still sealed, the tidbits of evidence against Clark that had been officially released by the authorities seemed fairly convincing. For example, there was the green-ink pen, with Clark's DNA on it, found under Le's dead body, and there was the DNA—again Clark's—on Le's body and clothing.

It appeared to most observers, then, that in due course, probable cause would be established; the case would go forward; and Clark would enter a not guilty plea to the murder of Annie Le. And after that, it was most people's strong belief—even before a trial was held—that Clark would be found guilty of murder.

So much for innocent until proven guilty.

FOURTEEN

It was a crisp New England morning, Tuesday, November 3, when Raymond Clark was scheduled to appear once again in the New Haven Superior Court, this time for the probable cause hearing. Photographers camped outside MacDougall-Walker Correctional Institution, where Clark was being held, were ready to take a picture of the man on his way to the courthouse. But they ran into bad luck.

Clark did not leave his cell or appear in court. The camera crews were greatly disappointed.

At 2 p.m, during a five-minute hearing in front of Judge Fasano, Clark's public defender Joe Lopez requested more time to make a decision as to whether or not to request a probable cause hearing. He said that the defense team had still not seen all of the evidence against Clark. The prosecutors agreed.

At the end of the hearing, Fasano agreed to delay Clark's probable cause hearing and set the court date for December 21. He stated that he expected to make his ruling on the sealing or unsealing of the warrants by Friday, November 6—three days away.

On Wednesday, November 4, Clark's fiancée, his sister, and his brother-in-law returned to work for the first time since September 11. Hromadka and Denise and Shawn Kent first met with Yale's human resources department to discuss ways in which the university could help them as they performed their jobs. None of the three had been accused of anything, after all, but they were well aware that publicity was not in their favor. After the meeting, it was determined that Shawn would be relocated from 10 Amistad to the Boyer Center for Molecular Medicine, a few blocks away.

None of the three made any public statements. Although a Yale official described the three as "bystanders" upon their return to work at Amistad, public opinion was decidedly different. Many in the Yale community felt that Clark would never have been hired at Amistad if his relatives hadn't vouched for him—and that having so many people from the same family working in the same building was problematic. And, their return to work after the murder was even more so.

One person, named "disturbed" on the Internet, wrote at 7:10 p.m. December 4, 2009, that he/she was surprised that Yale allowed Clark's extended family to return to work. The person claimed to have seen Jennifer "walking through my workplace laughing loudly without a care in the world. Around a similar time, I would see a person close to Annie sitting in a daze looking like she might burst into tears. For the sake of Annie's friends and colleagues, I wish Yale would move Ray's family members further away from the medical campus."

Of course, anyone can post a comment on the Internet. If this one comment was true, it was indeed upsetting.

FIFTEEN

As promised, on Friday, November 6, Judge Fasano made his decision public as to whether he would keep the warrant documents sealed, or if he would allow the public to read what was contained in them.

In a much-anticipated statement, Fasano said he *would* release the documents, saying that the public had the right to see them in an effort to "promote openness and transparency in the criminal courts."

The ruling was a win for Guggina and his clients, the *Hartford Courant,* the *New Haven Register,* the *New York Times*, and the AP. Very soon, the public could see the arrest warrant, and not long after that, they could look over the search and seizure warrants. Surely, they believed, this was in the interest of the public's right to know.

The judge added that most of the information in the documents had already been made public, although some new information would come to light. However, he said, some sensitive parts of the documents would remain confidential and that a redacted form of the arrest document only would be unsealed and be available to the public on Thursday, November 12. Fasano said that he would keep under seal "his written conclusion justifying the specific redactions." The search and seizure warrants, he stated, would continue to remain sealed until November 18.

As soon as the rulings were made public, lawyers following the case weighed in. David Rosen, LAW '69 and a senior research scholar at Yale, was quoted in the *Yale Daily News* as saying, "The conflict between free press and fair trial has been pretty intense at times and this case shows exactly why. People who are in the middle of one of those stories feel as though their own personal tragedy is overwhelmed by the magnitude of public curiosity and appetite for true crime stories."

Several criminal lawyers argued that since a jury trial could still be over a year away, and since the public had a short memory, releasing the documents would not unfairly bias a jury.

Some lawyers stated that although this case might seem like a clear case of the public's right to information versus Clark's right to a fair trial, they felt that that wasn't the case at all. In fact, they believed that the media's interest in the case, as voiced by Guggina, was an economic one. "My guess is that their bottom line is selling papers," said local criminal defense lawyer Nicholas D'Amato. "It's all about whether or not they can sensationalize a story and it becomes a commercial success for them."

Although there were now three days before the judge would release the arrest warrants, giving the defense time to appeal Fasano's ruling if they wished, public defender Lopez said he did not think they would. Guggina said he was considering his options as to whether or not to appeal the ruling. Obviously, he was upset because not *all* of the information was going to become public.

Because Wednesday, November 11, was Veterans Day, a state holiday in Connecticut, the arrest warrant application was released on Friday, November 13. It had been signed on September 17, two long months prior.

As soon as reporters got their hands on the affidavits, the headlines told the story:

New Haven Independent: Annie Le Warrant: Bloody Boots Read "Ray-C"

Yale Daily News: Bloody clothes, DNA led to Clark's arrest

Hartford Courant: Affidavit: Green Pen, Bloody Sock Had DNA From Annie Le and Raymond Clark III

ABC News on-line: Cops Watched Ray Clark Scrub Floor Drain at Yale Murder Scene: Evidence of Violent Struggle Between Annie Le and Her Killer

AP: Yale suspect's floor scrubbing raised suspicions

At the *Yale Daily News,* Vivian Yee, staff reporter, got her hands on the documents. Her headline in the paper read: "As investigation unfolded, suspicion of Clark grew." Her article summarized what was contained in the arrest warrant: when and why the authorities first came to suspect Clark; what Clark did on September 8 and on the following days; how the authorities pored over videos, collected over 250 pieces of evidence and interviewed over 150 people; and how Clark's DNA was linked to that of Le's. The thirteen-page arrest warrant, which contained two redacted sections, was signed by Detective Scott Branfuhr, a twenty-year veteran of the New Haven Police Department and lead detective on the case; Sergeant Alfonso Vazquez; and Judge Brian T. Fischer.

The warrant application began, "On September 8th, 2009 at approximately 10:40 p.m., Yale University Police Officers responded to 188 Lawrence St. Apt 3 New Haven CT to investigate a missing person complaint."

It continued by detailing Clark's encounter with Sergeant Wood on Thursday, September 10, stating how Clark moved the box of wipes and scrubbed a seemingly spotless floor.

Information that had not previously been made public included that a toothbrush and a maxipad were taken from Annie Le's house at 188 Lawrence Street and that DNA was extracted from them. After testing was done, the samples from Le were found to match the DNA extracted from the blood spatter on the box of wipes, as well as blood on a lab coat found at 10 Amistad.

The affidavit detailed that on September 12 police had found the following suspicious items in the Amistad basement: a glove and low-cut white sock, hidden within a drop ceiling; a pair of Viking brand boots, with one boot missing its laces; and one blue, short-sleeved scrub shirt—all having bloodlike stains on them. The affidavit noted that the bloody-looking boots were labeled "Ray C" and that the scrub shirt looked similar to a shirt worn by Clark, as seen in the surveillance video.

The affidavit reported that someone had attempted to clean blood off the walls in rooms G22 and G13, and confirmed that in G13, there was a "possible medium velocity bloodlike spray pattern." Further, the report verified the rumor that DNA from the sock found in the drop ceiling had been found to include a mixture of both Raymond Clark's DNA and Annie Le's DNA.

The warrant went on to describe how on September 13 the detectives noted an "odor similar to that of a decomposing body" and how they subsequently found a female inside a chase, with blood smears all around. After the following sentence, "It was observed that insulation was removed from the inside opening of the mechanical chase concealing the body," the next four lines were redacted, approximately fifty-four words.

The only information *not* redacted about the condition of the body was the fact that Le was found wearing "surgical gloves with her left thumb exposed." Clearly, there was something about the condition of the body that the court did not want made public.

The warrant listed the items found in the chase along with Le's body: a green pen, a stained lab coat, and a sock which was "similar in shape, color, and size to the previously mentioned blood-stained sock that was found on top of a drop ceiling in the North Hallway outside of the lab."

The next paragraph included information about the autopsy. It stated, "Dr. Carver, the Chief State of Connecticut Medical Examiner, performed the autopsy, and determined that the manner of death was a Homicide and the cause of death was strangulation." The next line, approximately twenty-six words, was redacted, and it appeared that this redacted portion might have to do with other details concerning the cause of Le's death. Specifically, there was no explanation for all the blood found at the scene of the crime or the violence that must have caused that blood to be shed.

The warrant went on to document the key-card swipes of both Clark and Le in the weeks leading up to September 8 and on September 8, noting anomalies in Clark's swipes on the eighth compared to previous days.

The report confirmed that Clark was the only person who used a key-card to access room G22 after the victim entered G13. In G22, investigators found physical evidence that included a cleaning spray bottle with bloodlike stains, two small round reddish beads, hair fibers, and "possible aspirated blood stains on an interior wall. . . . Hair and bloodlike stains were also found in rooms G13 and G33."

The report also noted that three people accessed room

G13 after 10:11—after Le had entered—on September 8, although it does not state the times they entered the room: Larry Godfrey, Rachel Roth, and Hao Shi. Bennett's lab members included Hao Shi, Ph.D., Rachel Roth, graduate student, Annie Le, graduate student, and five others: Peter Burch, Hui Qin, Matthew Soulsby, Faith Mercan, and Lei Zhang.

The last paragraph stated:

"Wherefore, I believe that the above facts and circumstances establish probable cause that Raymond J. Clark III, a white male with the date of birth of 01/28/85 who resides at 40 Ferry St. Apartment 1a in Middletown, Connecticut has committed the crime of Murder in accordance with the Connecticut General Statutes 53a–54a on or about 09/08/09 and as such request that an arrest warrant be issued."

SIXTEEN

On November 18, when the search warrant affidavits used to search the body, house, and possessions of Raymond Clark III were to be released, the judge declared that they would remain sealed for two more weeks. In his decision, Fasano said that when the warrants were released, parts would be redacted. In most cases, he said, "Connecticut courts do not seal or limit disclosures of arrest and search affidavits beyond the investigative stages." However, he said, he felt it would be appropriate to withhold some information in this case for three reasons: "Some information was inflammatory; some would prove unfairly prejudicial to defendant; and some material constituted an invasion of privacy unnecessary to the public's understanding of the criminal process."

Finally, at 9 a.m., Wednesday, December 2, the "Affidavit and Application" for "search and seizure warrants" were released. They contained nine separate warrants and over eighty pages, with twenty-three redacted sections. In spite of the redactions, the warrants revealed a lot of information that the public had never heard before.

The first warrant was issued before investigators discovered Le's body and was signed on September 13 by Detective Scott Branfuhr, Detective Chris Perrone, and the Honorable Judge Joseph A. Licari Jr. The warrant stated that the undersigned have "probable cause to believe that certain property . . . contained within 10 Amistad St. Yale Animal Research Center basement level . . . constitutes evidence of the following offense or that a particular person participated in the commission of the offense of Assault in the Second degree 53a–60."

New information revealed in this warrant included that after Le was reported missing, authorities called all the area hospitals, but that Le was not in any of them; that Sergeant Vazquez viewed video of the main entrance of 10 Amistad showing Clark passing through these doors "wearing blue scrubs several times" and "at 1554hrs, Mr. Clark was seen exiting these doors wearing a dark colored baseball cap, a dark colored shirt, and jeans."

The judge requested that the warrant not be released to the "owner, occupant or person named therein" "for two weeks from Thursday 9.13.09," citing, "The search is part of a continuing investigation which would be adversely affected by the giving of a copy of the affidavits at such time."

A second warrant, dated September 14, related to several items of clothing with bloodlike stains already seized from 10 Amistad. The warrant stated that these items constituted evidence of the offense of Murder 53a–54a—no longer Assault in the second degree, as was the case with the September 13 warrant. The evidence included a rubber glove; one low-cut white athletic sock; a pair of work boots with "Ray-C" written on the back; and one blue short-sleeved hospital scrub. The date of the seizure of these items was noted as September 12 and the purpose of the warrant was to obtain permission for their "examination, biological/DNA testing, and comparison."

A third warrant, dated September 15 and signed by Detective Sergeant Alfonso Vazquez, Detective Scott Branfuhr, and Judge Brian T. Fischer, included seven redacted sections (four, if one considered three concurrent paragraphs as one redaction). This affidavit was to search "the person of Raymond John Clark III, a white male, born January 28, 1985, Social Security Account Number (SSAN) 041-88-6137, of Ferry Street, Apartment 1A, Middletown, Connecticut."

The affidavit stated that certain items constituted evidence of Murder 53a–54a and were "within or upon a certain person, place, or thing," and requested permission to take saliva buccal swab samples; inked finger prints, palm and blade prints; body hair to include head and pubic hair; fingernail scrapings and cuttings; and photographs of Raymond J. Clark. (Later, Quinnipiac University law professor and former federal prosecutor Jeffrey Meyer stated that hair samples could "go to suggest there was a sexual assault of some kind.")

The document stated that the property would be submitted "to the State Forensic Laboratory for physical examination, biological and chemical testing, instrumental analysis, comparison, and reconstruction."

The first redaction, which constituted two lines, came after the sentence: "On September 12, 2009, Investigators from the Connecticut State Police Western District Major Crime Squad processed the lower floor at 10 Amistad St Animal Research Center for physical evidence related to this investigation." The next two lines were redacted, followed by these sentences: "Some items have tested positive for the presence of blood utilizing presumptive chemical tests. Particularly, investigators located one rubber glove . . . athletic sock . . . Vikings [sic] work boots . . . blue short-sleeved scrub."

The affidavit went on to note that "through chemical analysis, investigators uncovered bloodlike stains that had been cleaned off in room G22" and that "medium velocity bloodlike spray pattern [was found] on the wall of G13 which had been cleaned off." The next sentence stated that the stains were being tested and compared for "the presence of DNA by the State of Ct Forensic Laboratory located in Meridian." Then, the next three paragraphs were redacted.

A few paragraphs later came details that "a significant amount of evidence was seized from room G22: a cleaning spray bottle with bloodlike stains; two small round red necklace beads; hair fibers and aspirated blood stains on an interior wall." The affidavit stated, "Affiant Vazquez visually compared photographs of the two necklace beads found within room G22 and the necklace bead found within the clothing discovered with Annie Le's body, which appeared to be similar to each other." Then, the next five lines, an entire paragraph, were redacted, followed by: "A lab coat was seized from 10 Amistad Street and submitted to the State Forensic Laboratory for testing. The examination revealed that there was DNA profile from an unknown male and the DNA profile from Annie Le present on a few areas of the lab coat."

The affidavit then stated what the officers seized from the person of Clark upon executing the warrant. Among other things, buccal swab samples; fingernail scrapings and clippings; pulled pubic hairs; pulled leg hairs; pulled chest and abdomen hairs; pulled arm hair; pulled armpit hair; pulled eyebrow and eyelash hair; pulled head hairs; two sets of ink-rolled fingerprints; ink-rolled palm prints; digital photos of Raymond John Clark III; and one compact disc containing digital voice record of the execution of the Raymond John Clark III search and seizure warrant.

A fourth affidavit, also dated September 15, and signed by Branfuhr, Vazquez, and Judge Fischer was to search the home of Clark: "the Wharf Side Commons located at 40 Ferry Street, Middletown Connecticut apartment 40-1A."

However, new information in this affidavit stated that during this search and seizure, investigators located Le's email address within a locker labeled "Ray." It also detailed how surveillance video showed Clark entering Amistad at 7:05 a.m. on September 8 wearing "a black long sleeve jacket with white stripes and white sneakers" and a metallic man's watch. When leaving for the day, Clark was wearing a "black T-shirt and blue jeans."

A fifth warrant, signed on September 16, was for searching Clark's home and belongings a second time in an effort to find more evidence. New information in this affidavit included the fact that during a search of the 40 Ferry Street home of Clark, "blood like stains were located in plain view on the kitchen floor in close proximity to the entrance to the apartment." A presumptive test was performed and the bloodlike stains were, indeed, blood. *Whose blood was it?*

The affidavit also stated that on the previous day, officers had observed a pair of white sneakers with reddish stains, a blue garment similar to hospital scrubs, and a dark-colored garbage bag in or around the back seat of a red, two-door 2000 Ford Mustang registered to Raymond Clark of 1554 Ella Grasso Boulevard, in New Haven, Clark's home before he moved to Middletown. This warrant noted that the red Mustang was towed on

September 16 from the parking lot of Clark's apartment complex in Middletown to the New Haven Police Garage, where it was secured. When the vehicle was examined, other items of possible evidentiary value were found, including hairs, fibers, cell phones, and "one Walmart receipt from Lisbon, CT dated 8/21/09 for miscellaneous items as well as two fishing lures."

A sixth warrant, also dated September 16, noted that on Thursday, September 10, "investigators located a blue and black 'Outdoor Products' backpack containing a sock, monofilament line, and a fishing lure in room G6 of the lower level of 10 Amistad." (According to an article on NYDailyNews.com by Michael Daly on September 16, Clark came to work the day after Le went missing with a backpack, which was caught on the surveillance video. After it was revealed that inside Clark's backpack were wire, fishing hooks, and bubble gum, Daly wrote that Clark must have been planning to use those items in an attempt to retrieve his signature green-ink pen, which, according to Daly, Clark used to differentiate himself from others in the tech pack, from the space where Le's body was discovered.)

The affidavit added new information to the previous September 16 warrant. "On September 15, 2009," several items of evidentiary value were found at 40 Ferry Street: "a bait box with a clear top that contained fishing supplies, a reel of fishing line, and a package of fishing lures and lines." These items, it noted, were discovered on the floor of a kitchen closet. Two pairs of blue hospital-type scrubs were located in Clark's bedroom.

A seventh warrant, dated September 18, authorized the search of a second car, a 1999 red four-door Ford Taurus bearing Connecticut registration number 348-XKZ with vehicle identification number 1FAFP53U2XG108404. In this affidavit, there were two redactions about the vehicle, each of which would have shown to whom the vehicle belonged. Obviously, the court did not want the vehicle owner's name made public. *Was this to prevent a smear on the person's name if it turned out that he or she had nothing to do with the crime? Or was it to protect an ongoing aspect of the investigation?*

Startling new details were revealed in this affidavit about Clark's actions on September 8. Surveillance video showed that Clark left the front entrance of Amistad at approximately 3:54 p.m., wearing a dark T-shirt, jeans, white sneakers, and a dark-colored hat with a light-colored logo on it. He walked north on Cedar Street, and then entered a coffee shop at Cedar Street and Congress Avenue at 4:01 p.m. Clark sat at a table near the corner of Cedar Street and Congress Avenue with his fiancée, Hromadka, and an unknown female. They remained there for four minutes before leaving at 4:05. The three entered a 1999 red Ford Taurus, and the unidentified woman drove them away, with Clark in the front seat and Hromadka in the back seat.

According to the warrant, video footage then showed the three arriving at Clark and Hromadka's Wharfside Commons apartment parking lot at 4:35 p.m. "Subsequent surveillance of Clark revealed that he traveled quite frequently in this red Ford Taurus." After that revelation, the next sentence began, "A registration check revealed this car is registered to" and the next words were redacted.

The affidavit then stated that there was probable cause to believe that evidence for the crime of murder "will be found within the red 1999 four door Ford Taurus bearing Connecticut registration 348-XKZ."

Police seized the car, and soon seized and lab-tested

swabs of bloodlike stains, a plastic interior door panel, a plastic door kick plate, tan carpet, and two other sections of tan material from the car, all with bloodlike stains.

An eighth warrant, signed on September 23, stated that on September 20, night sanitation workers located a clogged drain at 10 Amistad. The Major Crimes Squad Central division responded and retrieved "medical scrub tops" stuffed into a drainpipe. On September 22, Amistad workers called the police after finding other items stuffed in a drainpipe "in the auto-clave room." There, investigators found "a large empty plastic bag, a white rag, tweezers, one scissor, and several Eppendorf plastic tubes." Because "these items were "past the debris collection basket," in order for someone to have placed them in the manner they were found in the drain pipe, someone would have had to "remove the debris basket and discard said items into the drain pipe."

The next paragraph recalled that as the investigators looked for more evidence in the clogged drain, they discovered a screwdriver sitting at the bottom of the pipe. Although a Yale University Sanitation Department worker, Barry Wong, noted on September 11 that the drain pipe was clogged, he did not report that until September 22, when he once again had problems with the drain. "In an attempt to clear the clog, he had plumbers clear the blockage which revealed the above stated items."

The screwdriver, tweezers, scissors, and Eppendorf tubes all raised eyebrows. *What role could each have played in the death of Annie Le?* The affidavit went on to say that even after extensive searches had been completed, some items of evidentiary value still had not been found: Clark's lanyard along with his electronic key card; a pair of dark-colored female mule-type shoes worn by Le on the day of her disappearance; shoelaces for one of the bloodstained work boots labeled "Ray-C" that were seized from the bathroom locker room; small reddish necklace beads from the necklace Le was seen wearing, some of which were found on Le's body; the black T-shirt, blue jeans, and black-and-white striped long-sleeve jacket that Clark was seen wearing on September 8; and a brown-colored leather computation notebook belonging to Annie Le.

The affidavit stated that due to these facts, they believed that "items of evidentiary value have been discarded throughout various points within 10 Amistad Street lower-level Yale Animal Research Center. For instance items of evidence have been found in ceiling tiles, laundry bags, secreted in walls, and in drain pipes. Furthermore the perpetrator has gone to great lengths to conceal evidence in multiple locations in unusual places. Some of these areas have been thoroughly searched and produced items of evidentiary value."

The search warrant gave investigators permission to search the Amistad basement further—specifically two women's locker rooms—in an effort to locate some of the missing items or any other evidence that might be linked to the murder. But, according a follow-up report on the search, "No items of evidentiary value were seized."

A ninth warrant, dated October 1, was for searching "all stored communication and/or files, email, internet activity, buddy lists . . . and telephone corresponding to an AT&T blackberry cellular telephone number (203) 848 0725." This affidavit stated that on September 12, 2009, "investigators for the FBI obtained a Federal Grand Jury subpoena for Clark's cellular phone (number above)." And on September 14, AT&T "sent the requested phone records to the FBI. Phone records showed that Clark made and received several phone calls on September 8," but nothing of great value was obtained. The records also showed that the BlackBerry had been used to connect to the Internet several times, but did not reveal what specific websites had been viewed.

The warrant authorized investigators to further search Clark's BlackBerry phone, which had been seized in the search of his home on September 15. The affidavit noted that "individuals who commit crimes will often times seek specialized information that will assist in the cleaning [of] blood and other body fluids found in a crime scene and/or hiding evidence of a crime. This type of information can easily be found on the internet." The affidavit also noted that experience showed that "person(s) participating in the commission of a a viole[n]t crime will take photos of the victim, the crime scene, and/or evidence of the crime and save them." A search of the content of Clark's phone—the websites he visited and photos he had stored—the investigators believed, could "produce evidence that will further link Raymond Clark to the murder of Annie Le."

The affidavit also stated, "the investigation has revealed that Raymond Clark has in the recent past contacted Annie Le through the Internet via email."

But the contents of that email were not shared.

SEVENTEEN

On December 3, the police requested a DNA sample from Clark's fiancée, Jennifer Hromadka. Her attorney, Robert Berke, stated that he was unsure why the authorities wanted her DNA, adding that in September, he was told that his client was not a suspect. He reported that also in September, investigators wanted to interview Hromadka, but that the interview never took place.

Experts began weighing in on why authorities would want Clark's fiancée's DNA. According to Dr. Bruce Goldberger, director of toxicology at the University of Florida, "Sounds like they have some DNA [and] they don't know who it belongs to. They're trying to rule her in or rule her out as a contributor to that DNA."

Berke stated that relatives of Clark began hiring lawyers as soon as Clark was named a suspect in the case. Clark's sister, Denise Kent, and her husband Shawn Kent hired lawyers. Clark's mother, Diane, also hired a lawyer, Ed Gavin, from Bridgeport.

Berke told the media that he received calls from Matt Lauer and Larry King, among over seventy other calls from reporters, asking for information about why there was a request for Hromadka's DNA. Recently, said Berke, Diane Sawyer sent flowers along with a request to interview Clark's mother.

Clark's public defender Beth Merkin and others stated that taking DNA from people close to the suspect was common in murder investigations. Because evidence could have DNA on it from several different people, police try to figure out who they are, so as to rule them in or out. Merkin also stated the DNA request would not change the defense's strategy for Clark. "Until I figure out how this fits into their theory, nothing changes from our point of view," she said.

State prosecutor John Waddock as well as New Haven state's attorney Michael Dearington declined to comment, as did New Haven Police Department spokesperson Joseph Avery.

EIGHTEEN

Although Raymond Clark was scheduled to appear in Judge Fasano's court on December 21, his appearance was put off until January 26 because, as Clark's lawyer Merkin stated, not all the evidence had been made available to the lawyers, so the court date for Clark had been "formally" continued. Merkin said this was not uncommon. "The starting point," she said, "is the lawyer to have discovery materials before we take any next step in any case." Merkin added that the prosecution was responsible for obtaining all the documents and evidence in question, and then to provide it to the defense. Waddock said his office was still waiting for reports from the state police lab because of a huge backlog due to retirements.

Lopez, Clark's other public defender, stated that he expected that all the necessary materials would be in his hands by January 26. However, the case could once again be delayed if he didn't have time enough to peruse all the materials.

Merkin said that on that date, Clark could enter a not guilty plea. If the public defenders felt that the prosecution had a strong enough case, said Merkin, "the defense would waive its right to a probable cause hearing."

After the hearing concluded, Connecticut State Police

spokesman Lieutenant Paul Vance vehemently disagreed with Waddock's statement about a backlog in the crime lab. "All the materials for the hearings to go forward have been made available." He said that the Le case was top priority and all the DNA evidence had been examined. Vance added that Waddock could be waiting for evidence in order to eliminate certain people through DNA, but that those reports would not change the case. Waddock disputed the fact that there was not a backlog saying the "sheer volume" of materials received caused delays. Vance did acknowledge that there was a backlog "to a certain extent."

Ira Grudberg '55, LAW '60, a trial lawyer, said postponing a court date is not unusual especially in a case "as serious and perhaps as complex" as Clark's. "It's totally normal," criminal defense attorney Paul Carty said.

PART
IV

ONE

On a cold and windy but sunny Tuesday morning, January 26, 2010, reporters flocked the Superior Court Building in New Haven. Charged with one of the most headline-generating homicides of the decade, Clark was expected to enter a plea—four months after his arrest—in Room 6A. The media was also there for another reason. On the third floor, jury selection was in progress for the triple homicide of Jennifer Hawke-Petit, wife of prominent endocrinologist Dr. William Petit, and their two daughters, Hayley and Michaela. The three were killed on July 23, 2007, during a home invasion in Cheshire, Connecticut, in which two accused men held all four family members hostage for several hours before ultimately setting the house on fire. Only William Petit survived the brutal attack. This case garnered a great deal of attention not only because of the heinous nature of the crimes, but also because it would be a death penalty case—due to the fact that it involved multiple murders. (According to the laws of Connecticut, the murder of Annie Le does not qualify for the death penalty. For a death sentence to be considered, the murder must meet one of several criteria; among them, the murder had to have occurred along with a first-degree sexual assault, or the murder had to have resulted in multiple deaths.)

Many reporters—from NBC, AP, the *Yale Daily News*, and other media sources—were seated in Judge Fasano's Superior Court, pads and pencils in hand, awaiting the arrival of Clark. This was the fourth court appearance in which Clark was expected to enter a plea. However, during each of the previous hearings, Clark's lawyers had asked for a postponement, citing that they and Clark hadn't had time to review the many boxes of evidence from the various investigative agencies involved in the case.

It was assumed that today Clark would waive his right to a hearing on probable cause and enter a pro forma plea of not guilty. But there was always the possibility that his defense attorneys would ask for yet another postponement.

At a few minutes after 10 a.m., Clark was led into the courtroom from a holding area, hands cuffed behind his back, legs shackled, and wearing sneakers and an orange jumpsuit. His hair was neatly coiffed, spiked, and very short.

Six marshals surrounded Clark as he stood straight, but with his head bowed, at the defense table. During the hearing, which lasted less than ten minutes, Clark responded with only a few words. Twice he said "Yes, sir, Your Honor"—once when asked if he understood that a new charge was being brought against him, and again when he was asked if he was voluntarily waiving his right to a probable cause hearing. The fact that Clark was waiving his right to a probable cause hearing meant that he and his defense team were conceding that the prosecution had enough evidence to bring him to trial on the charge of murder.

The prosecution was slapping Clark with a new charge as well: that of felony murder.

According to Connecticut law, specifically statute

C.G.S. §53a-54c, in felony murder, a person "commits or attempts to commit robbery, burglary, kidnapping, sexual assault, or escape and in the course of and in furtherance of such crime or flight therefrom causes the death of another person." In plain English, a charge of felony murder alleges that a person caused the death of another during the commission or attempted commission of a felony—such as robbery, burglary, arson, kidnapping, or sexual assault. (Any of the aforementioned crimes are referred to as the "predicate offense" in a felony murder charge.)

A charge of "felony murder" differs from a "murder" charge in that the former does not include the "intent" to cause the death of another person. To convict a killer of a murder charge, prosecutors are required to prove the death was caused intentionally. With a murder charge, if prosecutors fail to prove the killing was intentional, the conviction may be knocked down to manslaughter in the first degree, which carries a significantly lighter sentence.

However, with a *felony* murder charge, the prosecution must prove the defendant perpetrated a predicate offense (such as robbery) and that during the course of the predicate offense, a person dies—a lesser burden of proof than for murder with intent to kill. But the sentencing provisions for felony murder are severe.

During Clark's hearing, the prosecution offered no details as to what predicate offense they believed Clark committed that caused Le to die. In most cases, when a felony murder charge is brought, the prosecution states what the predicate offense was—and it is usually glaringly obvious: a robbery gone bad; a sexual assault; a burglary where the homeowner surprises the intruder and the homeowner gets killed. Despite the lack of detail, the new charge of felony murder provided some insight into the prosecution's tactics: If they couldn't get

Clark on murder with intent to kill, they intended to get him on felony murder—and they weren't letting him off with the lighter charge of manslaughter.

In addition to the new charge against Clark, there was another item of business. At the request of Clark's defense attorneys, Judge Fasano stated that he would permit the 1999 red Ford Taurus, which had been impounded months earlier, to be returned to its rightful owner, with the stipulation that the car could be later submitted as secondary evidence should it be needed. The vehicle had been impounded because it was in that car, at around 4 p.m. on the day Le went missing, that Clark, his fiancée, and an unknown female left a coffee shop and drove to Clark's home. According to documents, authorities had removed several parts of the vehicle, including interior plastic door panels and tan-colored carpeting that had bloodlike stains, and sent them for DNA testing. Nothing of evidentiary value had been located in the car, and therefore Fasano felt it could be released. The car belonged to Clark's mother, Diane—thus clearing up a mystery in the search warrants, in which the car owner's name was redacted.

Before the hearing ended, Judge Fasano stated that the court would reconvene on March 3 at 2 p.m., to discuss the possibility of unsealing the one search warrant that still remained sealed.

After the hearing, Clark's public defenders stated that Clark's spirits were "good."

Minutes after the court was dismissed, Clark's defense attorney Beth Merkin commented on the additional plea. She said that it offered another theory for the crime—besides intentional murder—ensuring that the prosecution "won't get boxed in."

Commentators also weighed in on what the new charge meant. Diana Perez of NBC Connecticut interviewed high-profile attorney Hugh Keefe, who was not personally involved in the case, and asked him to comment on why he felt the new charge had been leveled against Clark. The prosecutors, he said, have an alternative theory to present to the jury. That theory is "okay, he didn't mean to kill her, but he was attempting to sexually assault her or was sexually assaulting her, and in the course of that felony, she died." The new charge gives the jury another option, said Keefe. If the jury finds that the homicide was *not* intentional—in which case they couldn't convict Clark of the murder charge—they could still convict him for *felony* murder.

Keefe went on to surmise which of the felonies (predicate offenses) he felt the prosecutors believed Clark had committed. The only one that Keefe felt had even a remote possibility of applicability was sexual assault or attempted sexual assault. He felt that arson and burglary, for example, were not realistic under the circumstances.

Highly respected attorney Glenn Conway, who specialized in criminal defense law and served as a special public defender for the State of Connecticut in both its trial and appellate units, also weighed in on the hearing—although he, like Keefe, was not personally involved in the case. Commenting first on why he felt the prosecution brought the felony murder charge, Conway stated that there was a lesser burden of proof with felony murder. All that the prosecution had to prove was that the defendant committed or attempted to commit the predicate offense. "Intent," therefore, was no longer an issue. "With felony murder," said Conway, "a person commits a lesser crime, say kidnapping, and if a victim dies during the commission of that crime—although it's as serious as intentional murder—there is a lesser burden of proof."

Commenting on why he felt the prosecution might not

have stated a predicate offense during the hearing, Conway suggested that perhaps the state had expected this to be a sexual assault case, but when the lab results came back, the tests were less than conclusive. Therefore, reasoned Conway, the state may have decided to hedge their bets—to keep open as many options as possible.

Conway believed that simply charging felony murder puts the defense on notice, so they can't claim "surprise" later on. It's possible, he theorized, that the prosecution would later drop the murder charge and proceed with the sole count of felony murder. This strategy would stop the defense team from using an "extreme emotional disturbance defense." With a murder charge, the defense can try to convince the jury that the defendant was suffering extreme emotional disturbance while committing the crime—and if the jurors go along with this idea, they can convict the killer of the lesser charge of first-degree manslaughter, which carries a maximum sentence of twenty years. Under a *felony* murder charge, however, the law does not permit the use of an extreme emotional disturbance defense. "I think it's all about the State leaving its options open to get the greatest punishment with the fewest obstacles," said Conway.

Even if the prosecution proceeds with both counts—murder and felony murder—the jury would be instructed that evidence of extreme emotional disturbance on the part of Clark should not affect their deliberations on the felony murder charge.

"Each charge—murder and felony murder—carries with it a sentence of from twenty-five to life," noted Conway. "With either conviction, the expectation is for a number closer to sixty than twenty-five."

* * *

Because there was no mandatory time limit for setting a trial date, it was uncertain when Clark's case might go before a jury. In high-stakes cases, presiding judges do not force anyone to go to trial before he or she is ready, because were that done, appellate issues could result later. Although defendants have a right to a speedy trial, it is usually in their own interest that their attorneys have as much time as possible to prepare a good defense, meaning that it is not uncommon for high-stakes trials to be delayed for two to three years—or even longer.

But Conway pointed out, even though Clark has pleaded not guilty, he has the right to change his plea to guilty to some or all of the charges at any stage of the proceedings in order to avoid a trial and perhaps garner a lesser sentence, if the prosecutors agree. "This is his constitutional right," added Conway. "Suppose a plea bargain was worked out for forty years to serve, Clark may very well say to himself, 'At least I have a chance of seeing the light of day again.' If he goes to trial and loses on either charge, in all likelihood, he will never be a free man ever again."

TWO

With the January 26 pretrial hearing concluded and the new felony murder charge brought, the wheels of justice were grinding slowly forward. But as bureaucratic-seeming motions were brought forward and fine points of law discussed, everyone following this case was still wondering: *What* really *took place in the basement of 10 Amistad on the morning of September 8?*

With neither the accused, his lawyers, the police, nor anyone else personally involved with the case talking, it fell on the shoulders of savvy attorneys to offer a sequence of events based on known data.

First, the facts.

Clark was uncharacteristically busy on September 8 in the lab basement. On that day, he:

- repeatedly used his key card to go in and out of laboratory rooms G13 and G22, and his entries into these rooms were in close proximity to each other.
- entered G13 five times (compared to one time in the previous two weeks).
- entered G22 eleven times (compared to three times in the previous two weeks).

• used his key card at Amistad a total of fifty-
five times between 10:40 a.m. and 3:45 p.m. (an
uncharacteristically high amount of key-card
activity compared to previous weeks).

Concerning specific rooms, according to the police
affidavits:

Le entered G13 at 10:11 a.m. Her key card was never
used again.

Clark entered G13 at 10:40:59 and again at 11:04:37.
(After entering G13 for a second time, Clark did not
use his key card again for 46 minutes.)

Hair and blood were found in G13.

Hair, blood, and one bead were found in G33.

A cleaning spray bottle with blood on it, two beads,
hair, fibers, and possible aspirated blood were found in
G22. All the beads found in the several locations (including G33) were found to be similar to those on a necklace
Annie Le had been wearing.

Clark was the only person to use a key card to access room G22 after Le's entry to the Amistad building
on September 8.

On September 8, Clark was assigned to maintain
animals in G13 (called the Bennett lab); G24; and G33
(called the Assessa lab).

According to the arrest warrant, on September 8,
Clark signed "RC" in green ink on the sign-in sheets—to
rooms G23; G25; G26; G7C; G13; and G33 (the search
warrant of September 16 lists slightly different rooms in
which Clark signed in using a green-ink pen and the
initials "RC": G23, G27, G25, G29)—up until 1:30 p.m.,
when he made his last green-ink entry, to room G07C.
The next entry after that was at 3:48 p.m. to room G26,
written in black ink.

* * *

When asked for a possible sequence of events for what *could* have taken place in the basement of Amistad on September 8, attorney Glenn Conway imagined the following scenario based on what was known as of January 26, 2010.

Conway reasoned that, because the prosecution did not name "sexual assault" as the predicate offense to the charge of felony murder, the State might be looking at another predicate offense possibility, and he felt it was—kidnapping.

According to Conway, kidnapping is a broadly defined offense. At one point in Connecticut, the act of forcibly moving someone from a couch to the floor could qualify as kidnapping. In the kidnapping scenario relating to the Clark case, Conway posited that Clark approached Le in Room A, something happened between them, something that Clark initiated. A violent altercation occurred rendering Le incapacitated but still alive. Clark transported Le ("kidnapped" her), taking her from one room to the next—i.e., something happened in Room A; Clark had to get Le out of there. He took her to room B. She's still alive. However, eventually she died, either from her initial injuries or from Clark's own hand in Room B. He didn't mean to kill her. He did not have the *mindset* to kill her. It happened inadvertently as a result of the violence that occurred in Room A. To cover up what had occurred, Clark took her to Room C, where he hid her in a wall.

To give this scenario more specifics, Conway imagined there was an altercation in room G13 between Clark and Le sometime after 10:40 a.m. on September 8. Perhaps Le and Clark argued over work rules. Perhaps Le threatened to expose Clark for stealing, for being extremely rude, or for other bad behavior. Perhaps Le rejected Clark's sexual advances or insulted him in some way.

Whatever triggered Clark's rage, things got physical. He may have struck Le with an object, causing medium-velocity blood spatter to hit the walls of G13. Perhaps Clark pushed Le and she hit her head. The blow could have knocked her unconscious or rendered her semiconscious.

Clark panicked. What if someone came into room G13? He had to move her. His goal now was to cover up what he had done. To do that, he had to move her to a lesser-used room. Ideal was room G22. He went back and forth between G13 and G22 many times before actually moving her, each time, looking for the best way to get her there and exactly where to put her once he got her there.

At ninety pounds, Le was light as a feather. He may have wheeled her on a steel cart, covered by a sheet—and therefore not attracting any attention—to room G22. Once there, again, Clark panicked. Maybe she was regaining consciousness. Maybe she was attempting to scream. Maybe he strangled her to keep her quiet. Aspirated blood was found on the walls. The blood could have come from Le's coughing after blood had seeped into her lungs.

Strangulation can take a long time. How did he do it? Conway wondered. With his hands? With a ligature, such as a shoelace, scarf, or rope, or maybe, even, with Le's own necklace? Did he press something down on her throat? Was she able to fight back? (The answers to the manner in which Le was killed are most certainly contained in the autopsy report, which the authorities have not released.)

Now, Le was dead, Conway posited, and Clark's goal

was to get rid of all signs of what he had done. Clark was pretty good at cleaning up. Suppose he sprayed cleaning fluid on the bloody wall of G22 and wiped it off. He did the same in room G13. He did it so well, in fact, that no one noticed that the clean-looking walls had traces of blood on them until authorities used presumptive chemicals on the walls on Saturday, September 12.

Clark then went from one room to another, looking for an ideal place to hide the body. He came upon the perfect spot, in the locker room, behind the toilet, in a chase.

At 12:40 p.m., a fire alarm went off at 10 Amistad. Perhaps Clark set it off, thinking that while everyone was clearing out of the building, in those ten minutes or so, he could move the body to the locker room without anyone paying him any attention, and then he could hide the body. To enter the locker room, one had to open a door, and to enter the toilet area, one had to open a second door. Clark could have locked that door, while he was dealing with Le's body, so no one would have seen him doing the deed.

As people were leaving the building, Clark quickly removed the opening to the chase, along with some insulation within. He then went back to G22, wheeled Le out of that room and into the locker room. And while everyone was concentrating on getting out of Amistad during the fire alarm, he could have quickly stuffed Le's body inside the hole in the wall, placed the insulation back in on top of her, and then closed the door to the chase.

Le was now out of sight, Conway concluded.

It didn't take long.

In fact, after reviewing the blueprints of the basement of Amistad, it appeared that the distance between

G13 and G22—first walking past, on the right side, doors
to G11 and a mechanical room; then making a right
turn and a quick left past G18, and G20—was approximately forty-four feet: twelve feet directly north; two
feet west; then thirty feet north again to the door to
Room G22. Moving at a clip, one could easily cover that
distance in eight to ten seconds. So, without attracting
any unnecessary attention, Clark could have put a lab
coat over Le's body and wheeled her from G13 to G22.

To travel from G22 to G30g, which is the locker room
in which Le's body was found, Clark would have had to
have taken a longer walk. He would have exited G22 and
walked south, partway back toward G13, passing this
time on his left G20 and G18 and the mechanical room
(thirty feet). Then he would have turned right, walked
west to the other side of the mechanical room (forty
feet); turned north again, walked past G30h (twenty-two
feet), and then turned right, east, into the lobby off the
elevators, from which he could enter G30g (seventeen
feet). The total distance in feet: approximately 109 feet.
That could have taken approximately twenty-five seconds. Once inside G30g, it's approximately eight feet to
the toilet, and through a second door (which Clark could
have closed so no one would enter).

In both instances, if Clark was moving a cart with,
say, a body covered on the bottom shelf, no one would
even have taken a second look at him. Moving "things"
from one place to another was common as was moving
quickly. No doubt, everyone was intent on his or her
own thoughts regarding research or the fire drill.

Clark had to hurry to leave the building as the others were still filing out during the fire drill—and he
did, Conway concluded. Video surveillance showed him
leaving the building during the drill.

Even assuming Clark did what Conway imagined,

two small details would later come to haunt Clark. One, he was seen on the surveillance video leaving the Amistad during the drill with his head in his hands, apparently distraught; and two, he had visible scratch marks on his face and arms, which piqued the police's interest. When they asked him where he got them, he said they were from his cats.

Hmmmm.

THREE

With mounds of forensic evidence against Clark, many lawyers remarked that this would be a difficult case to defend. Some suggested that one tack would be to convince jurors that because police did not shut down Amistad immediately after the crime, the scene was contaminated. In this scenario, defense lawyers would have to go after how the evidence was collected, rather than the evidence itself, and most likely target the authorities and have them defend the decision not to seal the lab building. After all, the building was kept open for five full days after Le went missing. "You attempt to attack the investigative process as well as the conclusions," said William Dow III, a prominent New Haven–based defense lawyer, who was not representing anyone in this case. "If a jury is looking for something to grab onto," stated attorney Hugh Keefe, "then this could be something for them to grab onto."

In their defense, the police said that in the beginning, they didn't know whether the Le case was a missing persons case or something more sinister. The building was sealed, they said, when Le's body was discovered and the case was officially declared a homicide.

Several attorneys felt that even though DNA could be transferred in many ways, it would be hard to base a defense on issues concerning the problems with collecting DNA if, for example, Clark's DNA was found in the utility space where the body was located, and if Le's DNA was found on Clark's clothing.

When attorney Conway was asked, "Given what you knew on January 26, how would you defend Clark?" he said that he would probably try to get the murder charge reduced to a lesser charge, using an extreme emotional disturbance defense (EED), by establishing that all the violence occurred in a single room. "All of the EED evidence," he said, "would focus on the violence that occurred in Room A . . . evidence of a person snapping . . . a crime of passion." This would also serve to attack the felony murder charge by showing that no predicate felony had been committed. "I think that the state may have a problem nailing down exactly when and where Le died," added Conway. "This will create problems for them on the felony murder charge." If Le died in Room A, for example, a kidnapping could not have occurred. And if the state opted to proceed on the felony murder charge alone, prosecutors risked the possibility that Clark might end up going free if the jury did not buy the idea that a predicate felony had led to Le's death.

In spite of the strong forensic evidence against Clark, the lack of apparent motive could present prosecutors with a dilemma at trial. Jurors, like all of us, want to know *why?* And that was a question that investigators had yet to answer.

FOUR

On March 15, Judge Fasano released the final search warrant, dated November 25, 2009. In it, authorities sought saliva samples from Clark's fiancée Jennifer Hromadka. According to her lawyer, Bridgeport criminal attorney Robert Berke, Hromadka gave the requested samples after being served with the warrant. The warrant, signed by Detectives Scott Branfuhr and Alfonso Vazquez, stated that police had found a lanyard belonging to Hromadka when they raided the apartment where the couple lived, in September. The lanyard had Hromadka's DNA on it. Investigators wanted to see if Hromadka's DNA matched an unknown female's DNA found on the green-ink pen and an ankle sock, located with Le's body. In requesting the warrant, the detectives wrote, "Obtaining a confirmatory DNA sample from the source of the DNA found in these items will help investigators prove or disprove any involvement [she] may have had in the murder of Annie Le." Also, according to the warrant, Hromadka did not use her keycard to access 10 Amistad between September 8 and September 13, but police sources stated that some employees often followed others into the building, thus not having to swipe their own keycards.

Several words in the warrant were redacted. "Saliva

buccal swab samples from Jennifer Hromadka, a white female [a few words redacted], and to submit such property to the State Forensic Laboratory for physical examination, biological and DNA testing. . . ."

Hromadka has not been accused or charged in the murder and police chief James Lewis stated that Clark was the only arrest the authorities expected to make.

According to news reports, Hromadka continues to stand by her man, visiting him in jail regularly.

FIVE

What was it about disappearance and death of Annie Le that captivated so many? Was it that it was a mystery within a mystery? That every time a question was answered about the case, more questions were raised? Or was it just plain sensational?

During the week following Annie Le's disappearance, beginning on September 14, network TV programs spent one-third of their total news time covering the story. The Pew Research Center reported that approximately one-quarter of the public followed the story, while 12 percent followed it more closely than any other story that week.

Starting on September 10—two days after Le went missing—and continuing through September 21, Nancy Grace devoted most, if not all, of her eight shows on CNN to the Annie Le murder. It was one "bombshell" after another, as she delivered her breaking news each evening.

Stories about Annie Le were featured in *People* magazine and the *National Enquirer*. *New York* magazine printed a color-coded timeline infographic of the events, noting which news organization picked up the story and when. Reporters from cable news networks and daily presses around the United States streamed into

New Haven to get front row seats at every news conference.

The *New York Post,* Fox 61-TV, the *Hartford Courant,* the *New Haven Register,* WFSB-TV Hartford, the *New York Times,* and the AP were only a handful of the organizations that reported on the case daily. Le was the top link on Google News.

What was it about the missing person Annie Le, then the homicide victim Annie Le, that took the nation's collective breath away?

For some observers, it was a media-driven fascination—with nothing but crass calculation behind the coverage. "Journalists almost everywhere observe this rough rule of thumb: Three murders at a Midwestern college equal one murder at Harvard or Yale." This adage of journalistic wisdom was posted on the Web by Jack Shafer in an article titled "Murder Draped in Ivy," which appeared in *Slate,* an online political and culture magazine. According to Shafer, the press went "bonkers" over the Annie Le case—by September 17, the article stated, the *New York Times* had published five articles; the *Boston Globe* at least six; the *Washington Post* at least three briefs from the Associated Press; and even the *Times of London,* published several articles. It was a murder that "sold."

Echoing the sentiment that a murder at Yale or Harvard is always hot news was columnist MariAn Gail Brown, a reporter for the *Connecticut Post* in Bridgeport: "What gets all of us about Le's tragic slaying is that it involves not just any university student, but an Ivy Leaguer. Translation: Someone who might earn beaucoup bucks. Someone who possesses sky's-the-limit potential. Vivacious and attractive, too. Someone even the most critical parent could be hard-pressed not to like. . . . Nobody in the Elm City's 'hoods has that kind of cachet.

Are they worth less? Why don't their disappearances merit day-in day-out coverage like Le's? . . . The folks in the 'hood don't begrudge the attention Le's homicide is getting. They just wish somebody'd pay the same attention when their kids disappear, get shot or killed."

It's true that people disappear every day, people are killed every day, and not all disappearances and deaths garner the same attention. A murder at a university that multiple U.S. presidents have attended certainly attracts more. But it was not *simply* because the murdered student attended Yale that the nation was riveted. It was also because Le was beautiful, and she was brilliant. She was talented, and she was generous. And, she was a very-much-in-love bride-to-be.

But there was even more that kept the nation on the edge of its seat. As the investigation went from a missing-person case to a homicide investigation, the tale that unraveled became truly shocking. There were numerous lurid details. Gore—blood-spattered on the walls and an attempt to clean it up; blood on clothing and on shoes; blood all around the body. There was the allegation of a previous rape, coupled with possible rough sex. And then there was the unspeakable horror—a petite young woman stuffed into a wall that housed pipes.

The story had everything: youth, privilege, beauty, romance, sex, and depravity.

The only thing the murder didn't have was a satisfying explanation. *Why would Clark—or anyone—kill Annie Le bright and early on a Tuesday morning?* The crime just didn't make sense.

SIX

Then again, when did the murder of anyone make any sense? In mystery tales and television dramas, there's almost always a motive. Greed. Revenge. Jealousy. And unless the murder was carefully premeditated, there's usually a trigger. Rejection. Humiliation. Panic. Irresistible opportunity.

Three other cases had eerie similarities to the Le murder. Two involved Yale students, while the other did not; but they all involved a heavy dose of rage.

The first took place in the 1970s, when colleges were becoming increasingly sensitive to their obligation to minority students. After John F. Kennedy first termed the phrase "affirmative action" in 1961, employers, college deans, and others began taking pains to ensure that every applicant, worker, and student was being treated equally, without regard to race, creed, color, or national origin.

It was most likely in the spirit of affirmative action that Yale University accepted Richard Herrin, son of a single, Mexican-American mother who lived in *el barrio,* a poor neighborhood in Los Angeles. Herrin had attained excellent grades in high school and was valedictorian of his class—seemingly against all odds. Urged to go to college by his teachers and counselors,

Herrin applied to many prestigious universities and was accepted by nearly all of them. However, only Yale awarded him a full scholarship, so it was to Yale that he decided to go. In the fall of 1971, Herrin entered the privileged world of the Ivies, a world he later labeled as "so foreign he might as well have been transported to another planet."

While at Yale, Herrin began dating seventeen-year-old Yale freshman Bonnie Garland, graduate of a prestigious prep school and daughter of a Yale alumnus. For three years, the relationship blossomed. The two were practically inseparable and seemed to be poster children for the adage "opposites attract." In time, however, the relationship hit a rough patch. During summer break in July 1977, Herrin surprised Garland by showing up at her parents' home in Scarsdale, New York, an upscale suburb that was home to the wealthy and privileged. Garland asked him if he'd like to spend the weekend at her house, and without hesitation, he accepted. Perhaps they thought that this time together would bring the magic back into the relationship. However, after spending time exploring the neighborhood, meeting friends, and discussing their situation, Garland decided that Herrin was not the man for her. She wanted out of the relationship and told him so. That news did not sit well with Herrin.

After spending several restless hours in bed that night in the luxurious Garland home, Herrin searched for a weapon, found a claw hammer, and snuck up on Garland as she slept. He then bludgeoned her to death with four blows to her larynx and skull, which "broke open like a watermelon," Herrin later stated. On the ceiling, brain tissue was recovered.

Sneaking out of the house, Herrin slipped into the Garland family car and drove around for several hours, until he decided to stop at a church. There, Herrin confessed to the priest, "I just killed my girlfriend." Within hours, Herrin was arrested for murder.

It seemed like an open-and-shut case, with few people, if any, coming to the defense of the brutal murderer. However, an unlikely faction rose up and sprang to the fore. A group of Catholic clergy from Yale raised money to give to Herrin for bail and for his defense at trial, as well as for tuition for enrollment into another college under an assumed name. Following the clergy's lead, hundreds of members of the Yale community spoke up for Herrin, characterizing him as a misunderstood youth—a poor ghetto kid who was traumatized by the ways of a cruel and insensitive society—and mocking Garland for the manner in which she had treated him. After all, they declared, wasn't Herrin an illegitimate child and the victim of a poor upbringing in a minority neighborhood, *el barrio*, in Los Angeles, while Garland—well, her life of privilege didn't need much edification.

After being free on bail for nearly a year, Herrin was finally put on trial for murder in June 1978 in the Westchester County Courthouse. With a brilliant defense pitted against an equally brilliant prosecution, the trial's outcome was very much in doubt. After the high courtroom drama ended, the jury struggled for four days to come up with a verdict. Was Herrin guilty or not guilty; not guilty by reason of mental disease or defect; guilty of murder in the second degree; or guilty of manslaughter in the first degree.

On Sunday, June 19, Judge Richard J. Daronco asked the jury: "How do you find Richard Herrin under the first count, murder in the second degree?"

The jury foreperson responded, "Not guilty, Your Honor." There was an audible gasp. Garland's parents nearly collapsed with grief, while Herrin supporters felt nervously uplifted about the outcome thus far.

On the next count, manslaughter, the judge asked the jury foreperson, "How do you find Richard Herrin under the count of manslaughter in the first degree?"

"Guilty, Your Honor," replied the foreperson.

The Garlands felt some small amount of comfort—after all, Herrin had gotten away with murder, but not manslaughter. However, others felt differently. The verdict divided not only the courtroom but the New Haven community and the entire nation as well, which had been following the case closely.

Ten days later, on July 29, Judge Daronco handed down his sentence to Herrin: eight and one-third to twenty-five years with eligibility for parole after eight years. Most courtroom observers believed that this was an exceedingly "light" sentence, and they felt it was due to mitigating circumstances—Herrin's background and his emotional distress, along with Yale's uproar in his defense. Had Herrin been found guilty of murder, his penalty would have been twenty-five years to life. For the manslaughter verdict, however, he could have faced from one year to twenty-five years.

Herrin was paroled in 1995 after serving two-thirds of his time, nineteen years, in prison. He was forty years old.

A book, *The Killing of Bonnie Garland: A Question of Justice,* published in 1995, was written about the murder. Among other questions the author, psychiatrist Willard Gaylin, posed were: What role does psychiatry play in the courtroom and does the *why* of a murder mitigate a defendant's guilt? Another book, *The Yale Murder*, by Peter Meyer, pointed out the vast differences between the two young people both socially and geographically and then posed a similar question: Was justice truly served?

Until they met at Yale, Herrin and Garland occupied totally different stratospheres—but by the end of their relationship, they were eternally, bloodily bound together. Love had curdled and turned to hate.

Unlike Herrin and Garland, Annie Le and Raymond Clark were never romantically involved. But murder is an intimate act. By all accounts, Le and Clark passed each other in the Yale hallways—separated by inches, but divided by their workplace and societal roles. They were an unlikely, even impossible, match. And yet, they too may be now bound together by an unbreakable, undeniable connection. Clark's DNA was found on Le's clothing—the clothes she died in. He appears to have wiped her blood from the walls. Clark may have been the last person Le saw before she died.

A strikingly similar crime to that of Annie Le, although not a high-profile case, was that of the disappearance and death of Eridania Rodriguez. Rodriguez was reported missing on July 7, 2009, after not returning home from work. She was employed as a cleaner in a downtown Manhattan office building—and had told her relatives that someone was bothering her at work and that she was scared. An intensive search ensued—and ultimately Rodriguez was found on July 11 four days after she went missing, bound and gagged in an air duct in the building on Rector Street where she worked. Like Le, Rodriguez died at her workplace, and of asphyxiation.

Elevator operator Joseph Pabon, twenty-five, was arrested on Friday, July 17. He, like Clark, had a troubled past with a woman. Clark had been accused of forcing his high school girlfriend to have sex, although he was not arrested. Pabon had been arrested for choking his girlfriend. He had also been arrested for hurling a bowling ball through his girlfriend's car window in what was described as a blind rage. While questioning him, police saw scratches on Pabon's neck and hands. Police saw scratches on Clark's chest, face, and arms.

According to the medical examiner's office, DNA matched Pabon to the Rodriguez murder, just as it did Clark to the Le murder. In the Rodriguez case, both Rodriguez's and Pabon's DNA were found on a workman's glove found at the crime scene, just as Clark and Le's blood were found on a sock and other items of clothing in the lab basement.

The murder of Eridania Rodriguez took place just two months before the murder of Annie Le. It was as if killing women at work and stuffing their dead bodies into the walls was becoming a trend.

In 2000, a young medical student at Yale witnessed something that still haunts her to this day. In fact, it caused her to quit medical school. The woman's then boss pinned one of his workers against the wall and continually punched her in the face: "There was blood everywhere. He went into the most violent rage that I'd ever seen in my life." The medical school student who witnessed this was at her desk, only a few feet away. Although she has refused to give her name or the name of the professor involved to the media, her story was confirmed by both a current employee at the medical school and by Yale's clerical workers' union.

Workplace homicides have been investigated and analyzed by numerous agencies and professionals over the years.

According to a February 25, 2010, article titled "Reality and Its Discontents: Anger, Rage, and Workplace

Violence," by Dr. Stephen Diamond, forensic psychologist and expert on anger, evil, and destructive behavior, "Violence and mass murder in the workplace is a growing problem here in America." He wrote that the "rage epidemic" has hit the workplace especially hard.

Echoing this sentiment, the website "Workplace Violence Headquarters," a training and consulting resource to help protect the workplace from violence and rage, reported, "Workplace homicide is the fastest growing category of murder in the U.S. And homicide is now the leading cause of on-the-job death for women (and second-leading cause for men)."

The U.S. Department of Justice labeled the workplace "the most dangerous place to be in America! The problem is so pervasive that the Centers for Disease Control has classified workplace violence as a National Epidemic."

Statistics bear out the dire reports. The Bureau of Labor Statistics' Census of Fatal Occupational Injuries (CFOI) reported that there were 11,613 workplace homicide victims between 1992 and 2006. Averaging just under eight hundred homicides per year during those fifteen years, the largest number of homicides (1,080) in one year occurred in 1994, while the lowest number (540) occurred in 2006.

The National Institute for Occupational Safety and Health (NIOSH) reported that "homicide is the leading cause of injury death for women in the workplace, accounting for 40% of all workplace death among female workers. . . . Over 25% of female victims of workplace homicide are assaulted by people they know (co-workers, customers, spouses, or friends)."

However, even with those dire statistics, there is some good news. Overall, the 2008 preliminary U.S. workplace homicide count of 517 represents a decline of 52 percent from the high of 1,080 homicides reported in 1994, according to the National Institute for Occupational Safety and Health, and a decline of 18 percent from 2007, according to the Bureau of Labor Statistics.

According to Anne B. Hoskins from NIOSH, "bitterness," which she defines as a "chronic and pervasive state of smoldering resentment," is not only "one of the most destructive and toxic of human emotions," but is a primary cause for workplace violence. Other causes for workplace violence, including workplace homicides, are anxiety, anger from frustration or humiliation, and stress.

Everyone who was following the Le murder and had convicted Clark in their minds wondered what was the *specific* cause of her murderer's rage on that September morning. Was it bitterness due to his "station" in life? Was it anxiety about losing his job? Could it be frustration at Le's apparent indifference to him? Might it be the stress that came with being a lab tech?

Perhaps it was none of the above. Or maybe, it was a combination of all of the factors. If only Clark would talk, then *perhaps* the question would be answered.

EPILOGUE: SO MANY QUESTIONS

As of the printing of this book, many crucial pieces of information have not yet been released to the public:

the Annie Le autopsy report;

whether or not DNA was found under Le's or Clark's fingernails;

if the DNA in the blood on the walls of lab rooms G13 and G22 belonged to Le;

how the body was transported between rooms in the Amistad basement;

why a scissor, screwdriver, tweezer, and Eppendorf plastic tubes were hidden in a drain;

what the source was of all the blood in the basement, if the "only" cause of death was "traumatic asphyxiation due to neck compression";

how Clark got defensive wounds on his body if Le was found with her hands in plastic gloves with only the left thumb exposed;

whose blood was "in plain view on the kitchen floor in close proximity to the entrance to [Clark's] apartment"—seven days after the murder.

And then there are the other questions:
What was the motive for the crime?
Why was Annie Le targeted?
And finally the most basic question of all:
What causes someone to kill another person?
Perhaps the answers to all these questions will become clear when the case of the State of Connecticut v. Clark, CR09-97102-T, Connecticut Superior Court, goes to trial and a jury of Clark's peers reaches a final judgment on his guilt or innocence. Or perhaps the answers will remain forever sealed in the lightless places where only killers tread. Until then, the law presumes Raymond Clark III innocent until proven guilty.